The Principal's Guide

to

Teacher Personnel Problems

in

The Elementary School

The Principal's Guide
to
Teacher Personnel Problems
in
the Elementary School

Wayne

L.

Herman

Parker Publishing Company, Inc.

West Nyack, New York

PRINTED IN THE UNITED STATES OF AMERICA
70087—B&P

To my wife DOROTHY
and sons DOUGLAS and DEAN

Preface

Personnel problems can be as troublesome and perplexing to the elementary school principal as any he faces in the performance of his many duties. Often the manner in which he handles them will determine his own success as well as that of the educational program he directs and manages. This book considers a wide variety of specific personnel problems elementary school principals confront, and offers practical solutions which incorporate the best of both traditional and new procedures and thinking. Principals will find it a valuable tool in resolving the personnel problems of individual teachers, those arising between teacher and principal, teacher and teacher, teacher and pupil, and teacher and parent, as well as those with the non-professional staff. Throughout, the attempt is made to view a problem from the point of view of both principal and teacher.

The format makes for easy reference: statement of problem, discussion and analysis, and guidelines for action. The latter will prove especially practical for the busy administrator whose time is limited.

Addressed primarily to principals, assistant principals, and those aspiring to be principals, the following pages will be of interest and value to everyone involved in the improvement of elementary school administration including teachers themselves, superintendents, boards of education, parents, and professors and students in teachers colleges. Students in elementary school, of course, will not read it, but it is my hope they will be its prime beneficiaries.

It is impossible to name the many people with whom I have had the opportunity to work over the years and whose counsel and example have contributed to the writing of this book. Their names would fill several pages. However, I must acknowledge my debt to them. I am particularly indebted to Mrs. Dorothy Sizemore Smith for proofreading the manuscript and offering invaluable suggestions for its improvement.

Table of Contents

3. CURRICULAR PROBLEMS *(Continued)*

4. PROBLEMS INVOLVING DISCIPLINE AND DUTIES

6. Teacher Abuses and Negligences (Continued)

7. Non-Professional Personnel Problems

The Principal's Guide

to

Teacher Personnel Problems

in

The Elementary School

1

Principal-Teacher

Relationships

Daily the principal relates to his teachers. For the most part he deals with individuals, but occasionally he faces the entire staff. He knows the role he should play, but sometimes his concept of that role conflicts with the expectations of his teachers. Although he has a fine rapport with most members of his staff, one or two teachers occasionally cause him trouble. There are a few teachers whom he likes very much on a personal basis, but there is one teacher whom he secretly dislikes. While nearly all of his experiences on the job are pleasant, there are a few incidents now and then that cause sleepless nights.

Most of his teachers are women, and three or four are extremely emotional. Most of his teachers do not have strong philosophies and thus are easily influenced. Two teachers have out-of-date ideas about elementary education. One group of teachers likes shady jokes, another group is religious, and one teacher is an atheist. There are two cliques: one is composed of teachers who live in the local school community, the other of teachers who live in a town five miles away. Half the staff are

1

teetotalers while the other half, mostly the younger ones, enjoy an occasional drink. All want higher salaries, but while some want increments solely on the basis of experience, others are willing to work for raises by taking graduate courses.

In this community of individuals with different personalities, backgrounds, and points of view, the principal must be able to relate in ways which will receive both individual and collective approval and support.

AUTHORITARIAN VS. DEMOCRATIC VS. LAISSEZ-FAIRE RELATIONSHIP

> *"I sense that my teachers do not agree as to how I should play my role as principal. Some teachers expect me to make all the decisions; others want to have a voice in operating the school; a few teachers are interested only in their work and want to be left alone. How do I meet these varied role expectations?"*

When a principal first comes to a job, he will do well to be alert to the various roles his teachers will expect him to play, the general dominant expectations as well as the individual ones. His predecessor often can provide him with clues.

The challenge a principal faces is to cope successfully with all these different role expectations, for just as the principal wants his teachers to meet the individual differences of the students, so does the superintendent want his principals to relate satisfactorily with teachers.

It has been suggested by some writers that the teachers who want an authoritarian leader are the older teachers who were raised in a family where their father was the dominant and unquestioned household figure. This was the time when the platitude "children should be seen and not heard" was an accepted view. Other writers suggest that those desiring democratic modes of administration are mostly the younger teachers who as children had an equal vote in making family decisions. A few teachers are placed in still a third category. They are the ones who neither want nor encourage any direct supervision by the principal. Some consider these to be the highly creative types, but it is very difficult to generalize without a great deal of additional information.

Specific instances and conditions will dictate when the principal is to be an authoritarian, democratic, or laissez-faire leader. However, in the past decade the principalship, like the leadership post in many other fields, has undergone a distinct change. The authoritarian type of administrator has been supplanted by the democratic leader. In some graduate schools, prospective school administrators are taught about the peer relationship of principals—that the principal and his teachers are peers in their professional relationships. A good rule of thumb is to allow the staff a voice in issues or matters which directly affect them.

There are many valid reasons why a principal should exemplify democratic patterns of interaction. The democratic leader reflects and extends the type of society we live in. Also, since many minds are better than one, the combined resources of a staff strengthen a school's operation, and by permitting teachers to have a voice in determining policy and direction, the principal gains better support for the whole school program.

Suggested Guidelines:

1. Determine to meet the different role expectations of teachers.

2. Be flexible; let specific instances dictate your relationships with teachers.

3. Let the tenor of your relationships with teachers be unmistakably democratic, especially in matters which directly affect them.

PEER RELATIONSHIP

"I know a principal who has excellent rapport with his teachers. Everybody, including the principal, is on a first name basis. I understand this kind of relationship is called a 'peer' relationship. What is the proper way for a principal to relate to his staff?"

The concept of the peer relationship is now being introduced by some writers in the field of administration. The success of this concept in practice depends mostly on the personalities of the principal and teachers involved. Some principals with gifted personalities are well-suited to the peer concept of administration, but most of us have to work constantly at human relations.

Today because of the influence of trends which emphasize democratic administration, the principal is considered the leader of a team. All the players on the team, including the leader, are professional colleagues. However, leaders have individual personalities which determine the varying ways in which they deal with people. Unless you are fortunate and have a golden personality, it is probably better to visit only occasionally in the teachers' lounge, and avoid the use of first names.

Suggested Guidelines:

1. Always relate to the staff in a professional manner.

2. Let your experience and personality, together with "staff feedback" as to what they think of you, dictate the relationship you establish. Don't expect a double standard. If you call them by their given names, expect and accept their use of your first name.

3. In the course of a grave dispute with a teacher, it is absurd to revert to the use of "Mr." when you've always been on a first name basis.

4. Consider yourself an equal team player, but never forget you are a leader who must persuade and influence other team members.

CHAIN OF COMMAND

"I would like to have teachers discuss problems with me before they go to the superintendent with their complaints. How can I encourage teachers to respect the chain of command?"

The principle of the chain of command works well in some organizations but very poorly in others. In organizations composed of educated and professional people, it rarely appears to operate well because the chief administrator is always pleased to discuss a problem any staff member might have. No principal likes to learn of a staff member's problem from his superintendent. In industry, the assembly line worker would find it difficult to bypass immediate superiors and get to the plant superintendent.

I have, however, one suggestion that may encourage a stronger adherence to the chain of command. Discuss with the staff the importance of bringing complaints to the principal before going to the superintendent. State that if you as principal can not handle the problem to the teacher's satisfaction, you will recommend an appeal to the next higher authority; but also make clear to the complainant that, out of professional courtesy, you would like to be notified if and when an appeal is to be made. At the same time, tell the staff that when a parent brings a complaint to you about a teacher, you will immediately refer the parent to the teacher so that an attempt can be made to resolve the problem at the teacher's level. If the problem cannot be resolved at this level, then the principal will talk to the parent, and notify the teacher as to the result of the parent's appeal.

Suggested Guidelines:

1. Recognize that in practice the principle of the chain of command operates poorly in educational systems.

2. Encourage the use of the chain of command for the principal as well as for the teachers.

3. Tolerate teacher appeals to the superintendent and to board members.

School Philosophy

"I recently read that each school should develop a philosophy. Aren't most school philosophies about the same—general, ambiguous, and nebulous?"

It is most important that each school have a philosophy. It should be spelled out in clear and forceful terms. It should provide the guiding principles for all that happens at the school. All phases of the school program should be geared toward a realization of the precepts stated in the philosophy.

Although some philosophies are weak, a weak one is better than none at all. A reputable school will have practicable and specific items in its philosophy. A philosophy need not be long. Short statements that express what is believed and practiced are sufficient to make clear the school's direction and purpose. Here is one example.

Retentions:

1. A child who is being considered for possible retention will be analyzed according to the following criteria: social, emotional, physical, and intellectual development.

2. The nurse, the child's immediate prior teacher, his present teacher, and the principal will comprise the committee that studies the child and makes the final decision.

3. No child shall be retained more than once in the primary unit (Grades 1—3), and no child more than once in the intermediate unit (Grades 4—6).

4. Parents will be notified in a letter signed by both the principal and the teacher, by April 15, that their child is being considered for retention.

5. Parents will be notified by a letter signed by both the principal and the teacher by June 1 of the committee's decision to retain or promote the child. If the child is to be retained, the principal will arrange a conference with the parent. One committee member will be present at this conference.

6. If possible, the child who is retained will not have the same teacher the next year.

Other sections of this school's philosophy include such topics as corporal punishment, homework, meeting needs of children, and reports to parents. This last section defines the meaning of the grades A, B, C, D, and F.

Conflicts occur when a school has no philosophy. Differences of opinion cause friction. Shortly after a principal arrives on the job, he, along with the staff, should develop a written philosophy. It can become a part of the teachers' handbook. Revise it as the need arises.

Suggested Guidelines:

1. Develop, with the help of your staff, a working philosophy for your school.

2. Treat topics in a specific manner.

3. Make it a part of the teachers' handbook; add topics as you see fit.

TEACHERS' HANDBOOK

"Is a teachers' handbook really necessary? My teachers do not seem to pay much attention to it."

In order to protect yourself from possible court litigation arising from charges of negligence, you should have in writing certain operating policies and schedules regarding such things as: recess, lunchroom, bus supervisory duties, field trips, leaving the school grounds, defective equipment, injured or ill child, corporal punishment, and many others.

A handbook gives structure to a school's program. It reflects the thinking of the staff and the administrator. It is a handy source of reference. A proven charge of legal liability can hurt you badly, so put school policies in print. Do not rely on the spoken word. Give teachers a written copy of the summation of faculty meetings. State in the handbook that these summations are to be appended to the handbook. In a court case, it is every man for himself. Your strongest defense is that you have a specific policy in black and white in a handbook, and that every teacher has a copy of it.

Suggested Guidelines:

1. Develop a handbook immediately if you do not have one; not to have one is to live dangerously. Draft a handbook with the aid of a faculty committee.

2. Include operating policies and schedules; do not skimp on the contents. Too much is far better than too little.

3. Check each teacher's handbook during the summer to ensure that each one is up-to-date for the next school year.

4. Keep the handbook current; it is your armor, so keep it shining.

MORALE

"How can I give morale a lift in my school? The teaching is good but the morale is low."

Morale is an elusive feeling. Sometimes the personalities and attitudes of a few teachers seem to raise the spirits of others. Some school staffs seem to get it from their leader. Humor seems to spawn morale, as does security. Recognition and appreciation of teachers' efforts have a vital part in building confidence.

Examine the communication you have with teachers. Is it adequate? *Do* you communicate? Are the teachers aware of what is going on? Do you speak their language? Do you relate well to them? Do you consider yourself better than your teachers? If you do, you probably act that way. Do you try to use a pedantic vocabulary to impress them? Do you show genuine interest in their families? Do you ever engage in small-talk with them? Are you too serious? There are numerous things that affect morale, and the kind of climate or atmosphere we foster is a vital factor.

Publish a newsletter for the teachers. Most of its content can be about teachers—their classroom work, special projects, their families, their plans for the summer or future. Make it folksy and light. Select a "Teacher of the Month." Post the teacher's picture in a display case, with captions to describe his accomplishments. Have a Coke machine installed. Purchase a coffee percolator. Spruce up the teachers' lounge. Be optimistic in your attitude and outlook. Make the teachers feel that they are the most important people in the school system—for they truly are. How often do you use praise? How long has it been since you told your teachers—individually and collectively—that they are doing a good job, or that they did well on some specific school project? In the operation of your school are you a "slave to the book" or are you human?

Have a committee examine the topic of morale and prepare recommendations for its improvement. Often the teachers know the factors which cause low morale, and too often the principal is completely unaware of them. Provide a suggestion box for anonymous suggestions.

Suggested Guidelines:

1. Increase the humor level at your school; post cartoons about teaching with which teachers can identify.

2. Examine the way you relate to teachers; are you too serious? too rigid? trying to impress? taking too much of the glory?

3. Publish a newsletter for teachers about teachers.

4. Appraise the way your ship is run: humane or inhumane?

5. Select and recognize the "Teacher of the Month"; post his picture and cite his accomplishments.

6. Take a sincere interest in teachers and their families.

7. Let teachers know they are doing a good job; praise them for specific accomplishments.

8. Make teachers feel that any success of the school is due in a large measure to their efforts, because that is how it usually is.

FACULTY MEETINGS

"I dread faculty meetings because it seems we accomplish very little. Sometimes one or two teachers wreck a meeting. What are some guidelines which will bring improvement?"

A faculty meeting probably provides one of the most important opportunities for interaction between a principal and his staff. The manner in which a principal deals with group and individual behavior at this time will either enhance or impair his image with teachers. A course in Group Dynamics will do much to aid the administrator.

Regular meetings should be scheduled—perhaps on the second and fourth Tuesday of each month. But if there is no business to discuss, do not call a meeting. Cancel it. Of course, some faculty meetings will be of an in-service nature. When you schedule regular meetings, stay away from Monday and Friday. These are inconvenient times for all concerned.

Have the meeting in an informal environment, if possible. Do not choose a classroom. Unless all your teachers are petite and under five feet tall, the desks will not accommodate them. Serve refreshments. A cup of coffee and some doughnuts will do much to get the teachers into a pleasant frame of mind. Hand out an agenda the day before the meeting. This will give the teachers some time to think about the topics and will discourage rambling digressions.

All staff members should attend the meetings. Remember to notify the art, music, physical education, and foreign language teachers. If a topic deals with the domain of the custodian, be sure to invite him to the meeting as well. He knows more about his job than anybody else and rightfully should have a voice in a decision which directly affects him.

Recognize anyone who has a contribution to make. The more teachers verbalize, the better it is. Accept all ideas, even if they sound "way out." To reject an idea is to reject the thinking of the owner of the idea.

Strive for consensus. Stay away from voting if you can, for voting divides a staff. If you must vote, avoid hand raising; use the secret ballot. If the consensus is weak, discard the proposal. There must be strong support for programs, not just a feeble majority.

Discuss only those topics which affect the general school staff. Never spend time on a topic which is of concern to one or only a few teachers. If a teacher goes on a harangue about an isolated problem, interrupt her; tell her you will be glad to discuss it with her after the meeting.

And, most important, let the meeting be *short*. An hour is sufficient. Consider the members who have families and home responsibilities. If you have a full agenda, set definite beginning and closing times. Honor these times. If you fail to cover all the business, schedule a brief meeting for another time.

Suggested Guidelines:

1. Take a refresher course in Group Dynamics. Study how to deal with group behavior.

2. Schedule regular meetings on other days than Monday and Friday. If there is no business, cancel the meeting.

3. Use an informal meeting place. Serve refreshments.

4. Prepare and hand out an agenda a few days before the meeting.

5. Require all staff members to attend. Invite non-professional personnel if a topic concerns them or their job.

6. Invite and provide for teacher participation. Entertain all ideas.

7. Strive for consensus on proposals, rarely vote, and discard weakly supported ideas.

8. Discuss topics which interest and affect all teachers.

9. Don't have long meetings; an hour is long enough. Honor beginning and closing times.

In-Service Meetings

"My teachers complain about in-service meetings. They say the topics are too general. They think an in-service meeting should give them direct help with their teaching."

These are valid complaints. I have often thought the same thing. Some in-service meetings are planned around topics which are discussed on television or in periodicals. I have always thought that an in-service meeting should be directly concerned with the improvement of instruction. It should suggest techniques and stress new or different methods. It should give information about children and how they learn. It should provide depth and insight to topics teachers must teach. It should challenge. It should cause teachers to think about what they are doing in the classroom. It should give supporting rationale for what it suggests.

Some in-service meetings include all teachers, from kindergarten to the twelfth grade. If articulation, continuity, or curriculum planning is the topic, this is fine. But, aside from these topics, how much knowledge of method or content does a teacher of twelfth grade history share with a first grade teacher? Or, what does a seventh grade teacher of adolescents have in common with a sixth grade teacher of pre-adolescents? There should be specific in-service meetings for each grade level of the elementary school. Too often the expense of engaging speakers is prohibitive, but competent teachers in a district or county can also lead effective meetings; why not use them? It is not always necessary to have an outside speaker. This is one means of recognizing the exceptional or "master" teacher.

As more teachers directly participate in in-service meetings, the benefits increase. The common lecture-type meeting should be avoided; workshops should be instituted. There are many different ways to provide for effective in-service days. Abstracts of articles from scholarly journals can be read and discussed in small groups. Ideas can be gleaned from a visit to empty classrooms. Demonstration teaching and visitations to other schools are other possibilities. There may also be grade-level meetings and faculty in-service meetings.

Some kind of evaluation is necessary. Have the teachers do the evaluating. Encourage them to be honest in their evaluations so that improvements can be made.

Suggested Guidelines:

1. Be sure that an in-service meeting directly meets the needs of teachers.

2. See that the faculty has a major role in the planning, execution, and evaluation of the program; administrators should play an ancillary role.

3. Establish a format that provides for small groups of teachers with similar needs. Give opportunities for teacher participation and verbalization.

4. Occasionally hold mass meetings which concern articulation, continuity, and curriculum planning for teachers, K—12.

TEACHER ATTENDANCE

"How can I be sure that all the teachers in my school are present each morning? There are thirty teachers at the school."

No matter how many teachers are at a school, each morning a principal is obligated to know which teachers are present and which ones are absent. Principals learn through experience that they cannot depend on being notified by the teachers when they are going to be absent. Children have to be supervised by someone.

One of the easiest ways is to have teachers check in and out of the building each day. Develop a weekly form. It is not required that they write in the time they arrive or leave; only initial the IN and OUT spaces next to their name. By glancing at this sheet, a principal can quickly see which classroom needs supervising in case a teacher is tardy or absent. Place this Check In—Check Out sheet in a convenient location. Explain to the teachers that the only reason for the sheet is so that you can readily determine who is in or out of the building. Post all notices and announcements at this location, also.

Suggested Guideline:

1. Use a Check In—Check Out form which *all* teachers have to initial when they arrive and leave school.

TEACHER EVALUATION*

"The superintendent requires principals to make formal evaluations of all teachers once a year. What steps can I take to allay the fears of my teachers?"

In any field, whenever evaluations are made the criteria are established beforehand. How else could a fair evaluation be made? These criteria are characterized by definiteness and clearly discernible evidences. Even this is not enough, however. The people in charge of whatever is being rated invariably receive a copy of the criteria well in advance of the evaluation. Auditors treat company accounting departments this way. NCATE sends to colleges their criteria for accreditation. Professors define examination areas for their students. To be registered, an architect or an electrician knows the specific areas on which he will be tested. How else could one prepare for an examination?

Does the principal want his teachers to be prepared for his visit? Or does he want to try to catch them doing something wrong? Surely this should not be the purpose of his visit. Moreover, a teacher is rarely dismissed on the basis of one formal evaluation. Cumulative instances of misconduct or incompetence usually cause dismissal. Explain this to your staff.

*Parts of this topic and the following topic are used from the author's article, "Teacher Observation," *The National Elementary Principal*, 43:63-4, April 1964.

Develop in collaboration with the teachers themselves the criteria which will be used for these formal evaluations. Give each teacher a copy well in advance of the classroom visit. Unless the superintendent states otherwise, a formal evaluation should be conducted by appointment. Again, the day for auditing companies, accrediting schools, examining students, and qualifying artisans is almost always known in advance. One may think a teacher will pose as a paragon of instruction when he knows of your visit ahead of time. But teachers can never go beyond their training and experience. When a teacher knows of your scheduled visit, you see him at his best. Knowing the best a person can do, it seems to me, is better than knowing what his worst is.

When you visit the classroom, conduct yourself with the proper restraint. Observe social amenities. Greet the teacher when you arrive and say "good—by" when you leave. Move freely around the room, if it is appropriate. Do not act like a "Snoopervisor." To increase the reliability of your judgments, remain with the class a few hours. Thirty to forty-five minutes of observation will be sufficient for new teachers, since you already have a fairly good assessment of their ability from observations during the year.

Hold a conference the same day as your visit. This is imperative. Discuss each of the evaluative items and make cooperative judgments. Let the teacher do most of the talking. You won't learn anything if you do all the talking. Provide cues so the teacher can make most of the suggestions for change. The written report should include both positive and negative annotations. Encourage each teacher to append to the report his own comments. This serves as a safety value for some teachers and reveals more about the teacher to the principal. Also, the teacher may include valid rationale which clarifies or refutes a negative statement by the principal. The principal isn't always right, you know.

A week or two after the conference, the teacher should receive a typewritten copy of the evaluation. The teacher's signature should be on the retained copies. A follow-up of the mutually determined recommendations for improvement should be done about two weeks after the formal evaluation visit.

Suggested Guidelines:

1. Develop, with the staff, the criteria to be used in the evaluation.

2. Give each teacher a copy of the criteria.

3. Make appointments for formal evaluation visits.

4. Observe social amenities when entering and leaving classrooms.

5. Be helpful during the evaluation. Don't sit, watch, and record.

6. Have a conference with the teacher on the same day of the classroom visit.

7. Let the teacher append comments to the evaluative report.

8. Provide a typewritten copy of the evaluation for the teacher's records.

9. Follow-up mutually determined recommendations.

TEACHER OBSERVATION

"I don't seem to be able to get into classrooms very much. When I do go, the teachers seem nervous and edgy."

Probably many principals never observe classrooms in action more than a few times a year. Observing classroom performance is a distasteful job to some administrators; for other principals, it is a rewarding experience. Administration of the elementary school developed for the prime purpose of overseeing instruction. How can a principal faithfully fulfill this responsibility if he spends most of his time in places other than where instruction is going on?

The first step is to make a schedule for classroom visits. Suppose there are twenty teachers on your staff. If you visit one classroom a day for a period ranging from thirty to sixty minutes, you can visit all the classrooms in a month. Then repeat the schedule each month. Keep the same time for at least two months so that you can follow-up the first month's suggestions for change.

Talk to the staff about your planned visits before you put the schedule into operation. Convince them that your role as a principal includes being a consultant. Emphasize that your purpose is to offer help. In short, make it clear that you are not a judge and, therefore, you will not act like one. The success of the observation plan depends on your proven sincerity to do what you say you will do: be a consultant who will help the teacher.

When you enter the classroom, greet the teacher. If he is busy teaching, greet him with a hand gesture. Practice the social amenities when you leave the classroom, as well.

Adapt your behavior to what is going on. If the teacher is teaching directly, sit with the class. Never sit away from the class. This implies that you are there as an inspector, and who likes to be inspected? If the children are working at their seats or in small groups, move freely around the room. Make favorable comments to the teacher at the appropriate time—when you won't disrupt anything. Work with the teacher. Talk over what is going on. Don't broach a weakness or the children will sense that their teacher is lacking in skill. In case you are not able to talk with the teacher at this time, give her a wave and a smile as you leave. This will give her confidence in what she is doing. You will want to visit the teacher after school in her room this same day. This clears the board. If something needs changing, attempt to get the teacher to offer the suggestion. You can do this by providing hints. It is important that the teacher and the principal *agree* on changes. Avoid dictating—you will defeat your purpose. Persuade . . . influence . . . listen. Don't do all the talking!

The principal prepares an anecdotal record on the visit and puts it in the teacher's confidential folder. Next month when he visits the teacher, he will observe what progress the teacher has made.

Suggested Guidelines:

1. Schedule classroom visits, and be sure to honor the schedule.

2. Convince the staff your role is that of a consultant, not a judge. To convince *yourself* that this is your role may be still more difficult to do.

3. Observe the social amenities upon entering and leaving the classroom.

4. Hold an evaluative conference on the same day as the observation. If change is needed, give cues which will help the teacher to make

suggestions for improvement. He will be more inclined to carry out the suggestions *he* makes than the ones *you* make.

5. Keep an anecdotal record of visits in the teacher's confidential folder.

6. Follow up proposals for change at the next visit.

TEACHER INITIATIVE

"Sometimes a teacher will take the initiative and do something when, I feel, he should have first consulted me. What can I do to discourage this?"

It depends on what the teacher did. If it was something of a harmful nature, then the infraction should be listed in the teachers' handbook. If it was minor and something that needed to be done, congratulate yourself that you have teachers with initiative. In the course of each school day, there are numerous decisions that teachers have to make. Most of these decisions are relatively insignificant and should not concern you. If the teacher brings all or most of them to you, then your job becomes an onerous one. Besides, a principal is not always in the building to be consulted at the time a decision has to be made. Encourage teachers to think for themselves. Do not be afraid to delegate responsibility and authority. A good principal does not have to make all the decisions.

Suggested Guidelines:

1. Encourage teachers to make decisions and take the initiative in areas which directly affect only them.

2. As occasions arise, list in the teachers' handbook certain prerogatives which belong exclusively to the principal. Some examples include:

   a. Giving orders to the non—professional staff.
   b. Permitting use of the building to community groups.
   c. Charging requisitioned materials to the school.
   d. Taking a class off of the school premises.

Salary Increments

"What are some guidelines for administering salary increments? Some of my teachers seem to think they've been treated unfairly when salary increments are announced in May."

Unfair administration of salaries can destroy morale, even among those on the high side of the salary range. Salaries are always relative. It does not matter how much another school district is paying its teachers; what matters is how a teacher's salary compares with the salary of the teacher across the hall, or with a teacher in another school in the district, or even with a beginning teacher in the school system.

Teachers together with administrators should comprise the salary committee. The salary committee constructs a salary schedule which provides for experience, education, extra duties, military duty, and perhaps merit pay. The schedule is accepted by the school board and is distributed to all teachers. Each teacher knows what he has to do in order to qualify for increments. The administrator adheres to the schedule when hiring teachers, and the salaries of all new teachers are published in the newspaper. There will be no problem if the accepted salary schedule is honored.

There is, however, one more point to be considered. When there is an increase in the starting salary of beginning teachers of, for example, $200, then all increment steps on the salary schedule have to be increased by $200. This means that *all* teachers must receive a general increase of $200. Otherwise, each increase in beginning salaries causes inequities for every teacher in the system. If the district cannot afford to put all teachers where they belong on the new salary schedule within one year, all teachers in the example above could receive $100 a year for two years. This raise would be, of course, in addition to regular salary increments.

Suggested Guidelines:

1. A salary committee comprised of teachers and principals should draft a salary schedule.

2. The board of education accepts or revises the salary schedule.

3. Each teacher receives a copy of the schedule.

4. The salary schedule is adhered to by administrators. Salaries of the new staff are published.

5. Increases in beginning salaries result in general salary increases of the same amount for all teachers.

REWARDING TEACHERS WHO VOLUNTEER

"Whenever I ask for volunteers to do a special job, one of my teachers invariably volunteers."

There is within each human breast the need to be recognized by his fellow-men. The need varies with individuals. Humans do many unusual feats solely to gain recognition: a fellow will sit on top of a flag pole for a couple of weeks, a disc jockey will broadcast continuously for 72 hours, or twenty-seven and a half college boys will pack a public telephone booth.

Those who volunteer their services when there is no monetary reward are usually attempting to meet the need to be recognized. This need is very powerful with some people. We find it operating in all levels of life. Both the hobo and the "hobnobber" want to be recognized by their peers and colleagues. In the economic field the need is satisfied by conspicuous consumption. There is nothing inherently wrong with this motive, and often much good is done because the need for recognition exists.

Recognition is one of the incentives that lures people into teaching. Many teachers at all levels of instruction have some of the *show-off* in their blood, and that is why many of them are successful. Teaching is an art. Often a good teacher is also good in histrionics. Sometimes, he is a legitimate artist. All teachers need recognition from the principal—some teachers need a lot, but all teachers need some. What is one do about these needs? Meet them. Give the teachers recognition!

The need for recognition, as with most other needs, becomes stronger when it is inadequately fulfilled or constantly denied. The volunteering teacher has recognition pangs. Many workers have these pangs in varying degrees because superiors seldom take steps to alleviate or satisfy the need responsible for the condition. Since teachers are no different in this regard, general ways of giving recognition will be discussed.

The printed word is one effective way. Who doesn't like to see his accomplishments recorded in black and white? It gives a boost to the morale, and its effect is lasting. The paragraph, no matter how small it is, can be clipped out and shown to friends; it can be saved and reread a month, a year, or five years later. Each time it is reread the need for recognition is met. Begin a weekly school column in the local newspaper. The newspaper officials will welcome the news items, and there is seldom any charge. Each week, describe the special activities and projects of different classrooms, always listing, of course, the teachers' names. Let the size of your school dictate the number of teacher-reporters gathering news.

Initiate a monthly or bimonthly teacher newsletter. Use informal and humorous writing. Tell about the worthwhile things going on in the teachers' classrooms. Acknowledge the accomplishments of teachers and children. Adjust some of the news of the teachers' newsletter for a newsletter to parents, using the same kind of informative reporting. This is one way of giving recognition to teachers.

On the check-in-check-out sheet or on the teachers' bulletin board, call attention to a special job that has been well done by a teacher. There are numerous commendable projects going on in classrooms, projects which the editors of *Grade Teacher* and *The Instructor* would be grateful to have for their magazine. In special cases where exemplary service has been given, send a personal letter commending the teacher for his efforts.

Select a "Teacher of the Month." Display a large photograph of the teacher with accompanying citations on the bulletin board or display case near the front of the building. Have one of your teachers who likes photography take pictures of special assembly programs, activities or events. Photograph some of the interesting and unusual projects in classrooms. Display these photographs at a central location. Reimburse the photographer from the petty cash fund. Promote a special assembly program in which the children honor their teachers. Permit teachers to lead faculty meetings when panels, debates, symposiums, or question-answer discussions are held.

Every teacher can do something better than any other teacher. Find out what is his forte. Have your teachers write down what they can do best. At various times of the year give each teacher a chance to demonstrate his talent and instruct other teachers in his particular techniques.

Some teachers could be enrichment speakers for the school. They could present an auditorium program showing their hobbies, collections, kodachrome slides, or musical talents. At P.T.A. meetings, mention specifically the teachers who have done certain things worth recognizing. Spread the praise around—the teachers have earned it.

Suggested Guidelines:

1. Recognize that teachers who are performing artists on the stage of the classroom each day need and should have *applause*.

2. Use some of the following techniques to give recognition to teachers:

    a. The printed word: school news in the local newspaper, teacher newsletter, school newsletter for parents, posted compliments for special jobs well done, published articles in teacher journals.

    b. The picture: "Teacher of the Month" using teacher photograph with complimentary captions, displaying photographs of activities and projects sponsored.

    c. The spoken word: mention achievement of teachers in faculty meetings and at public meetings; cite specific achievements.

    d. Teacher leadership: teachers instruct other teachers in their *best techniques;* teachers present to auditorium gathering their hobbies, collections, slides, or musical talents; faculty meeting participation in debates, panels, and symposiums.

REWARDING SUPERIOR TEACHERS

"I have a highly skilled teacher who keeps abreast of current developments in the field of elementary education and who conscientiously applies this knowledge to her teaching: she visits pupils' homes, has an effective guidance program, provides for individual differences, does projects beyond the call of duty. How can I reward this outstanding teacher?"

Unfortunately, extra compensation for good teachers is rarely given. Two common ways to reward a superior teacher are to provide a salary differential and to take the teacher out of the classroom and promote her to an administrative post. There are a number of additional steps which can be taken; for example, the teaching load of this master teacher can be reduced. She can be titled Administrative Assistant for Instruction and can assist new or weak teachers in their planning and instruction. She can chair a school district committee on instruction which will offer suggestions periodically to the superintendent for improvement. The principal can encourage and promote the publication of accounts in teacher journals and in the local newspaper of worthy projects carried on in her classroom. She can be used for demonstration teaching purposes for the entire school district. Workshop involvement is another possibility. Encouragement can be given for conducting action research.

In the summer she can have a role in developing or revising curricular guides or in leading enrichment or remedial educative programs. You may think that all this special attention will have a deleterious effect on other teachers and will give the skilled teacher a "big head." Since recognition is given in every other field for outstanding service and competence, why should teaching be the exception?

You may want to nominate her for a medal of excellence for classroom teaching which is awarded by Freedom Foundations, Valley Forge, Pennsylvania. Certainly, informal acknowledgements to her on her achievements should be made by the principal or supervisor. The superintendent of schools can send her a letter of commendation, in which she is informed that a copy has been placed in her personnel records. Recognize her and other superior teachers at a formal dinner meeting attended by district teachers, administrators, and members of the school board.

Too often praise and recognition are withheld until a teacher retires or leaves a position. Since praise has a motivating effect on workers, the prudent principal will capitalize on its benefits.

Suggested Guidelines:

1. Provide a salary differential for superior teachers.

2. Reduce her teaching load and make her a helping teacher for new or weak teachers. Give her an administrative title.

3. Have her chair a district-wide committee on instruction which reports to the superintendent.

4. Encourage and promote publication of projects carried on in her classroom.

5. Use her for demonstration purposes.

6. Give her leadership responsibilities for workshops.

7. Encourage her to carry out action research.

8. Employ her in the summer for developing curricular guides or teaching remedial or enrichment programs.

9. Nominate her for a teaching award from Freedoms Foundation, Valley Forge, Pa.

10. Informally acknowledge her achievements. Ask the superintendent to write her a letter of commendation.

11. Recognize superior teachers at a dinner meeting for teachers, administrators, and board members.

12. Give cash bonuses.

TEACHER BY-PASSED FOR PROMOTION

"There is a teacher in my school who is interested in advancing into administration. The personnel committee doesn't have confidence in his ability to get along with other teachers. He is being by-passed for promotion this year. I think he has good potential. How can I explain the situation to him?"

Being by-passed for promotion sometimes happens to fully qualified people. There are numerous reasons: color of hair, neckties worn, jealousy, personality conflicts, playing favorites, or any reason imaginable. The important thing is how the by-passed person is handled.

If the personnel committee thinks he is a potential candidate for future promotion but needs seasoning, tell him so; and give him new respon-sibilities and opportunities in the school so that he may get this needed experience. If for some reason the committee seems to think the candidate does not fit into future plans for promotion, then tell him the truth. Give him the reasons. Avoid, however, attempting to build a case with picayunish instances as your only support. He will never respect you for this. Do not stifle his hopes, for we have neither the right nor the insight to say he will never be a successful principal.

Don't desert him. Help him pick up the broken pieces. Being rejected is a shattering and humiliating experience. If he has ambition, he will apply to another school district. Encourage him to do this. Help him to understand that school systems differ, as he may be an outstanding principal in another milieu. Point up his assets. Give him the names of a few placement agencies. Tell him you will be happy to give him a good reference. Make sure he knows he has your support.

Suggested Guidelines:

1. Give him valid reasons for being by-passed. Do not stack the deck against him to justify his being by-passed.

2. If his future remains bright with the school system, encourage his growth.

3. If his chances of future promotion are nil, encourage him to apply elsewhere. Suggest placement agencies. Speak optimistically about his chances of success in another school system.

4. Be a positive reference for him. When someone is knocked down, he sometimes needs help to get up.

DISCHARGING UNSATISFACTORY TEACHERS

"I have a teacher who is incompetent. What steps should I take to get rid of her?"

The decision that a teacher's employment be terminated should come only after unsuccessful efforts to make her a satisfactory teacher. Also, the decision to release a teacher should never be reached before there is sufficient cumulative evidence in the form of written annotated records on file.

Some principals put pressure on the teacher to resign by visiting her classroom daily and taking copious notes. This form of harrassment is clearly unprofessional. Although policies differ, cases are often treated on an individual basis. The below discussion could be used as a general guide.

First, the principal seeks support from the local school board or, in a large school system, from his immediate superior, to take action against the teacher. After he receives approval, the principal sends the teacher a letter stating that for the welfare of the school she should resign her position at the end of the year. If the problem is grave enough, she should submit her resignation within a specified time. Keep the school board or your immediate superior apprised of any developments. If she does not resign, send her another letter stating that if she fails to submit her resignation by a certain date, the school board plans to take appropriate action. State briefly that it will be in the interest of her own welfare to resign, rather than be dismissed. Be professional in all your contacts with her. If she still doesn't resign, the next action is usually a letter by the principal in which she is given a specified date and time for a hearing before the school board. The hearing is usually set for not less than thirty days after the teacher receives notice of the scheduled hearing. If the board decides to dismiss the teacher, which it will probably do, there is a possibility of further litigation in the courts.

Suggested Guidelines:

1. Make honest efforts to bring the teacher up to a satisfactory rating.

2. Apprise your immediate superior of the case and seek his support.

3. Send a letter to the teacher requesting her resignation. Set a deadline for the resignation.

4. Keep your superior notified of any and all important developments.

5. If the teacher refuses to resign, write another letter and give her another deadline, but tell her if her resignation is not received, the school board will find it necessary to take action. Point up the advantage of resigning as opposed to being dismissed. Be explicit in your letters. Let her know exactly where she stands.

6. Be professional in your relationship with the teacher.

CONFIDING IN TEACHERS

"There are two teachers on the staff who seem to understand some of the problems I face. I seem to be able to relax with them; our families exchange visits infrequently; and at these times we occasionally talk shop."

The question of whether a principal should confide personal school business to a teacher is easily answered by three words: NEVER! NEVER! NEVER! Usually a neophyte principal who violates this unwritten rule learns his lesson in a devastating, shattering, and never-to-be-forgotten manner. Do not confide to a teacher information about another teacher. She will think you confide to other teachers information about her.

In this and other ways the principalship is a lonely and friendless position which accumulates much information about teachers, problems, and circumstances which must remain for the most part in a sealed reservoir. To handle such information promiscuously is a breach of professional trust and ethics. It seems that people are prone to share with other humans delicate matters relating to their friends and acquaintances; nevertheless, those in leadership posts who would be successful in human relations must have sealed lips.

Suggested Guidelines:

1. Never discuss personal school business with any staff member.

2. If you feel an urge to talk shop with a teacher, discuss school business in positive terms.

3. Organize meetings with nearby principals for the purpose of

discussing common administrative problems. You will find them safe, beneficial, and therapeutic.

DISCUSSING TEACHER PROBLEMS

"Occasionally in a faculty meeting or in the teachers' lounge a teacher will broach a touchy topic which only affects her. How can I deal with these instances effectively?"

The discussion of a touchy subject should involve only the teachers who are directly concerned. To discuss an individual issue with the entire staff is to invite dissension, for staff members will be forced to choose sides. Sometimes a teacher will solicit votes for her side from non-involved teachers and attempt to railroad a decision in the faculty meeting. If the principal weakly tries to evade the proposed problem, he loses face and gives the impression he has no solution.

Immediately after the topic is raised by the teacher involved, the principal should state positively and firmly, "I would like to talk with you about this immediately after this meeting." Then go on quickly to another topic. After the meeting, tell the teacher you will be happy to discuss this problem with her in your office at her convenience.

Suggested Guidelines:

1. In the presence of other faculty members, never allow the discussion of touchy topics or isolated topics which do not pertain to the whole group.

2. Use individual or small group conferences to discuss these topics.

3. Be receptive, patient, fair but firm, lest disorder become the rule of the day.

RELIGION AND POLITICS

"Shouldn't topics of religion and politics be avoided in informal principal-teacher discussions?"

It depends on the principal and the teacher who discuss the topics. Even highly educated people have built-in biases and predilections for one side or another and these specific areas are strongly connected to their emotional systems. The best advise is to refrain from discussing inflammatory topics, if possible.

Suggested Guideline:

1. Don't court topics which have strong emotional overtones.

TEACHER'S TEMPER EXPLODES

"There are a couple of teachers on the staff who are highly emotional. Occasionally one of these teachers will come to me in a nervous state with a problem. Usually her temper explodes. Sometimes the invective is aimed at me; sometimes at another teacher, pupil, or parent. How should I handle these incidents? Both teachers are satisfactory teachers."

Unpleasant outbursts like this do occur, and it is surprising that they do not occur more frequently. Teaching is hard. Anybody who even baby-sits with thirty elementary school children for six hours has no easy job. Teaching is nerve-wracking. It is enervating. It is a continuous task of decision-making. Researchers who have observed classrooms tell us that teachers interact with children on the average of six or seven times a minute. This amounts to over 2000 interactions every school day. An interaction includes a nod of the head, giving permission to sharpen a pencil, asking a question, a smile, a grimace, and many more. Almost every interaction requires a decision: "Does Johnny really have to sharpen that pencil?" or "Should I ignore Sue's behavior? If I don't ignore it, what should I say to her?" or "What question on Mexico should I ask next?" On and on it goes, every day of the job. It's little wonder that teaching leads all other professions in the number of nervous and mental breakdowns.

Back to the problem of teacher outbursts. A smart principal will not try to equal or outdo the exploding teacher's volume. You were made a principal because your superiors thought you were outstanding in understanding people and in handling interpersonal relations.

The next time a teacher comes to you in a huff, try this. Listen to her. Do not say a word. Listen . . . listen . . . listen. Don't defend, admonish, or clash with her. This would make the temperature even higher. Think of the outburst as a safety valve for her, even if what she says is against you. Recall the tensions of teaching. Listen . . . listen . . . listen. When she stops talking, repeat to her exactly what she has said to you. Verbal behavior analysts call this accepting her feelings and ideas. When we are angry, we want somebody to listen and accept what we have to say. When you accept her feelings and ideas by paraphrasing them to her, her temperature starts to come down. For instance, you say something like this, "You are angry because the busses are always late and the children get boisterous and loud. You think the busses should be here on time." If she interrupts you, let her continue to explode. When she stops, repeat to her what she has just said. When the temperature is down to a comfortable level, you can begin working on a reasonable solution.

Suggested Guidelines:

1. Recognize that teaching causes many tensions.

2. Listen to the exploding teacher. Listen . . . listen . . . listen.

3. Repeat to her what she has just said when she stops talking.

4. Wait until her temperature is at a comfortable level before trying to work out a satisfactory solution to the problem.

TEACHER OFFENSE

"One of my teachers accused a student in front of the class of taking some money from her purse. The teacher had only circumstantial evidence. The parents of the boy came to me and demanded that the teacher apologize to their son in front of the class. How would you handle this and other tactless acts by teachers?"

When a teacher commits a mistake which is important enough to warrant correcting, the principal must deal directly with the teacher who is in error. Never mention in a faculty meeting that teachers are to take their attendance registers with them during a fire drill if only one or two teachers have violated the policy. Tell the teacher yourself in private.

When teacher offenses involve parents as in the above example, the principal has two broad responsibilities: to support the teaching record of the teachers and to rectify the situation to the satisfaction of the parents. You may not know anything about the case until the parents call or visit you. Take notes as they talk to you. Arrange a conference with the teacher and the boy, and with the teacher alone. Take notes as she talks too. Sometimes a comparison of the two sets of notes will uncover misunderstandings which will clear up the problem.

If the parents seem to be right, as in the case above, the teacher should be told that she had insufficient evidence to label the boy a thief in front of the class. Tell her that you understand how she could lose control of the situation and call the student a thief, but advise her to apologize to the boy in front of the class. Mention that you want her to meet with the parents and you in a brief conference at which time she can extend apologies, and assure her that you will support her teaching record to the parents at this conference.

Do not make the conference a formal affair. Have some cookies on a dish. Avoid dragging the conference out. If the teacher apologizes at the outset, the parents' offense is stymied. In the presence of the teacher, tell the parents what a fine teaching record the teacher has. Do not dismiss the teacher from the conference and give her the impression that behind her back you are going to disparage her action. End the conference on a positive note. Walk out of the office with the teacher and the parents.

Suggested Guidelines:

1. Deal with the offender; do not discuss teacher errors in a general way at a faculty meeting or when the errors concern only a few teachers.

2. Advise a teacher to take appropriate action to rectify the error.

3. Support the teaching record of the teacher when dealing with the parents. This should be done in the presence of the involved teacher.

4. Try to understand why a teacher made the error and take steps to prevent a similar error from happening again.

5. Recognize that anybody that uses a pencil doesn't have much of the eraser left on it.

PRINCIPAL OFFENSE

"I said something at a faculty meeting that I shouldn't have said. Should I apologize at the next staff meeting or just forget about it?"

Some leaders think that an apology weakens their image. This is not the case. Admission of an error has the opposite effect. It tells people that you think right. It cleanses. It makes things right. At some time or another everybody says or does something in error. We do not really believe that others think we are perfect. We do not believe it ourselves, so why not apologize? In order to preserve our image, we can't afford to do less. The mistake need not be magnified. Just say you were wrong, and you are sorry about it. People with character never hesitate to say they are sorry. They want to make amends with the people they have wronged. They, themselves, want to feel right inside.

Suggested Guidelines:

1. Recognize that you are not a demigod; everybody makes mistakes.

2. When you make a serious mistake or commit a significant error in judgment which affects a person or a group, make amends as soon as possible.

FAVORITES

"How should a principal treat teachers he especially likes? What about the teachers whom he dislikes?"

Some children attract and others repel their teachers; this is human nature. Similarly, teachers affect principals. But just as the good teacher will not display affection for some, to the humiliation and embarrassment of others, nor will the skilled principal give any indication of his affinities. He will treat all alike, including those he dislikes. This is a guiding principle of professional and ethical courtesy—in the church, in business, in society, everywhere.

In his personal and social life, a principal has the right to entertain anyone he chooses. This may certainly include favorite teachers and their families. But on the job, he must exercise discretion and accord all teachers equal and just consideration.

Suggested Guidelines:

1. Treat all teachers alike, professionally.
2. Exercise the right to select social and personal friends.

FACULTY SOCIALS

"Our staff is divided over the issue of wet and dry socials. What would be a good compromise? Also, a teacher suggested that the non-professional staff be invited to socials. Is this a good idea?"

At the outset, let me endorse social gatherings for teachers. Two or three socials a year can do more to foster good principal-staff and teacher-teacher relations than almost any other single type of event. A lark at the bowling alley, a picnic with a ball game, a gala dinner party, an overnight excursion—all permit us to let our hair down a bit and our colleagues come to realize we are human. But let us be careful. We are still *Mr. Principal.* We cannot act the fool and still hope to maintain and present an image worthy of respect and emulation. A social occasion is not a license to play loosely with sex or with the bottle. A sense of propriety is an earmark of the educated man.

The issue of "wet" or "dry" socials plagues many staffs. Some principals reason that if the party is "wet," the "drys" will not attend. If the party is "dry," the "wets" will attend with the real "wets" bringing their own bottles. It seems to me that whether drinking is or is not carried on at a social, as professionals representing and employed by a certain community we are obligated to deport ourselves in a way that will not damage our public image. Fun we can have, but some fun is clearly forbidden.

During the year it is important for the entire school staff—professional and unprofessional—to get together at least once. Bus drivers, custodians, and cooks are also members of the school team. Plan a social to which they may be invited. A team plays better together when the members know each other better. At other times during the year, the non-professionals and professionals may have their own separate socials.

Suggested Guidelines:

1. Promote faculty socials; they strengthen our understanding of colleagues.

2. Let *some* of your hair down, Mr. Principal, but not *all* of it!

3. Respect the views of the minority; seek a compromise between the "wets" and "drys."

4. Invite the entire school staff to at least one social during the year.

OBSCENE JOKES

"I know a principal who says that the jokes he tells increase his rapport with teachers. He says it shows he's human."

A joke or clever anecdote often releases tension, eases conflict or helps to get one out of a dilemma. It has the benefit of throwing everybody out of gear for a while. It's therapeutic. After the laughs, we can start over again or begin something new.

For adults, the rare joke does not concern sex. But jokes about sex can be on varying levels. And the level of our jokes is the important thing. Our jokes tell people where we stand—on the road, or in the gutter. Because of telling certain jokes, a few principals, not unlike some barbers, can never reclaim soiled impressions. Of course, a teacher is never to be made the butt of a joke.

Suggested Guidelines:

1. Use jokes, but be careful which ones you use. The principal is a professional leader, not a professional comedian of burlesque caliber.

PERSONAL PROBLEMS OF TEACHERS

"Does a principal have any responsibility to deal with the personal problems of his teachers?"

Yes, he has a very definite responsibility. Some of the larger companies provide counseling psychologists and psychiatrists for employees. They realize that many employees have personal problems, and that personal problems affect the quality and amount of productivity. To dismiss skilled workers with serious personal problems and hire and train new ones is costly. Besides, management takes the benevolent attitude. They feel that they have a responsibility to help workers who in turn have given them faithful service.

Life has its rain clouds for teachers. Sickness, injuries, death in the family, finance, and husband's loss of job are only a few. Often a teacher comes to the principal to seek counsel and solutions. Give whatever advice, assistance, consideration, or sympathy you can. Sometimes a teacher has to leave the job temporarily to take care of a sick husband, or for some other reason. Tell her that the job will be hers when she is ready to return. Hire a temporary teacher for the interim. Advise the school board to grant sabbatical leave to teachers with long service who need extended leave for illnesses or long recovery periods for sustained injuries.

In times of severe personal problems a person needs special support and understanding from an employer. Effective school policies are flexible policies. Stretch them for deserving cases.

Suggested Guidelines:

1. Give advice only when asked.

2. Encourage and assist the teacher who needs help. Stretch some

policies to keep the teacher on the job and payroll. Keep the job open for her if she has to leave temporarily.

3. Be particularly indulgent with disabled teachers who have given long and faithful service.

In The Family Way

"How long should I let a teacher work who is in the family way?"

Policies differ with school districts. For various reasons, I suppose, a teacher should suspend her teaching for at least four months before and after the birth. This is a policy which is usually set by the school board. To strengthen the policy, ask the teacher for a note from the doctor verifying her expected delivery date. Some school districts require the teacher to sign a form which releases the school board from any legal liability resulting from an accident on the job.

Suggested Guidelines:

1. This is a policy which is usually set by the school board.

2. Teachers should suspend their teaching at least four months before and after the birth.

3. A certificate from the doctor verifying the expected delivery date should be required.

4. Some school districts require that a teacher release a school board from legal liability resulting from an accident on the job during the pregnancy.

Tired Teachers

"There is a teacher on the staff who frequently looks and acts fatigued. What can I do to help her?"

When I had a child who looked tired or sleepy in class, I sent the child to the health room for a nap. *Academic learning can not occur until the most pressing need is met.* The same principle applies to teachers. The immediate response of a principal should be to let the teacher take a nap in the health room. Pinch-hit for her. But if the reason for her tiredness is due to personal neglect, one or two naps may be embarrassing enough to cause her to miss the late show on television or to reduce her activities on the social circuit.

Discuss the problem with her. It may arise from physical causes. Even though she is being treated medically, she may have to take a month off to recover her strength and health. An operation may be necessary. Perhaps her energy level is not appropriate to the early primary or late intermediate grade that she teaches. A teaching assignment with the third or fourth grade may solve the problem. Maybe she has taught the same grade level for too long. Perhaps she is bored—boredom and monotony engender tiredness. Change her teaching assignment. Maybe the thermostat in her room needs adjusting: it gets too hot in the classroom. It is possible that her class has too great a range of ability or individual differences for her to cope with, or that there are too many problem children. When you talk with her, encourage her to be honest with you. Tell her you want to help her. You have to find the causes of the tiredness; then you can take the appropriate action.

Suggested Guidelines:

1. If a teacher looks and acts tired, invite her to take a nap in the health room.

2. Discuss with her the reasons for her tiredness. Encourage her to be honest with you because you want to help her. Some reasons for a teacher being tired include:
   a. Views the late show on television.
   b. Has an hyperactive social life.
   c. Is physiologically weak in stamina.
   d. Has an insufficient energy level for the class she is teaching.
   e. Is bored with the same grade level she has had too long.
   f. Malfunctioning thermostat makes the classroom too warm.

g. Has too many problem children or a class with too large a range of ability or individual differences.

3. Take the appropriate action after determining the cause.

NERVOUS TEACHERS

"A few of my teachers are extremely edgy and nervous when I talk with them or go to their classrooms."

Perhaps a personal problem—one connected with the teacher's mode of living, occupation, marital status, or colleagues—is bothering the teacher. If so, its removal will effectuate a cure. The principal can have a conference with the teacher and state, "You seem nervous lately. You know I have confidence in your teaching, Mrs. Jones. I wonder if you have some kind of perplexing problem that's bothering you?" If she has a problem but does not wish to discuss it with you, at least you understand that a definite problem is the reason for her nervousness.

Probably, most of the nervous teachers have exhibited nervousness for a long time. These teachers cannot be cured we are told because they have an inferiority complex, and they have a generalized fear reaction to a wide variety of situations. Psychologists tell us that a total cure for chronic and habitual nervousness is seldom possible. However, any favorable change in the circumstances of the teacher or in the quality of his adjustment can serve to alleviate the condition.

Frequently the principal himself, whether he knows it or not, behaves in such a way as to make a teacher, any teacher, uncomfortable and insecure. He has a mien which exudes superiority. He comes into the classroom, sits at the rear of the room, observes, and writes notes on a pad, and later imperiously tells the teacher which changes to make. It takes even an extremely well-adjusted person to be unaffected by this kind of judgement. The principal has all the answers. His definitive and erudite answers to all problems maximizes the teacher's feelings of inferiority. Some principals prefer to have nervous teachers. Some honestly like being the despot because the teachers are afraid of them.

Even though some of these nervous teachers have been nervous most of their lives, there are some things a principal can do to reduce their anxiety. Build on their assets. Let them know you recognize their strong teaching areas. Give them opportunities to grow in their interest field. Build up their self-confidence. When problems arise in which they are knowledgeable, consult them for their opinion.

Develop a relationship with the staff in which the team approach—principal and teachers—operates in practice. Consider their opinions. Don't always have the right answer. Don't always correct their thinking. If the teachers are *off base*, feed them cues so they can correct their own responses. Then give them credit for helping to find right answers and right solutions. A good leader does not take the glory. He is wise enough to know that his followers need recognition and will grow and develop in a climate where praise is given. He does not give praise promiscuously. He is discriminate but not stingy in his use of it.

He does not try to make teachers uncomfortable because he appreciates the cordiality of his superintendent when they have conferences. When he detects nervousness, he puts the teacher at ease by using the right words or some pleasantries to ease tension. He occasionally has lunch with the teachers and sometimes engages in small talk with them before and after school. He treats them as professionals. He doesn't consider himself better than anybody else in the building but just part of a team. He is the leader of the team and when decisions are to be made, he recognizes that several heads are better than one.

In short, the principal sets the climate of a school. He can change some of the circumstances which will cause teachers to be nervous. The right atmosphere can help the habitually nervous person to develop more confidence and feel less insecure.

Suggested Guidelines:

1. Recognize that a personal problem may cause nervousness.

2. Recognize that chronic or habitual nervousness is difficult to cure.

3. Establish a school climate where a democratic and friendly partnership between the staff and the principal exists. Some hints are:
   a. Build upon the assets and strengths of nervous teachers.
   b. Allow the teachers to advance proposals.

c. Don't always have the ready answer or the learned explanation.

d. Distribute praise freely but discriminately.

e. Make teachers comfortable in your presence. Avoid the *boss* image.

f. Be interested in teachers as persons. Show an interest in their families and in their goals.

g. Don't think you are always right. Consider teachers' opinions and feelings.

SPINSTERS

"There is a spinster on our staff who seems to have a chip on her shoulder. She is disagreeable to the children and unpleasant to most staff members."

A principal must be careful not to attribute immediately these short-comings to the fact that the teacher is unmarried. Being unmarried and being disagreeable often do not go together. You and I both know many unmarried people who are personable and well-adjusted, and we know some married people who are ill-tempered and weak in human relations.

The teacher may have personal problems which make her irritable. Since the children and the staff are affected by her attitude, you, the principal, have the responsibility to have a conference with the teacher and to discuss your observations. Ask her if she has any problems with which you could help her. Your sincere and helpful interest should be evident. If she is convinced of your sincerity and trustworthiness, she will probably welcome the chance to share with someone the burdens she is carrying.

She may have no personal problems; it may be her manner which is caused by a negative outlook on life. She may feel that other people are not interested in her. A solution may lie in the teacher feeling wanted and needed by someone or by some organization. Take a special interest in the spinster. Develop this solicitude with discretion. Discover her interests. Bring her newspaper clippings or show her magazine articles in her interest field. Give her a definite responsibility for some area of the school program, such as director of visual aids or school librarian. She should be one of the hostesses when the faculty has a social. Invite her and another teacher to accompany you and your family to the theatre or to a special event.

As principal, you could discreetly introduce the spinster to the leader of a local woman's organization; encourage her to become a member. Indirectly you could suggest to the students or to a student's parent that a surprise birthday party be given for the teacher. Also, you should display a genuine need for and appreciation of her services. Whatever you do should be done with discretion and with the purpose of giving status to the spinster.

Suggested Guidelines:

1. Take a kindly, discreet interest in the spinster. Discover her interests; then capitalize on them.

2. Give her a definite responsibility for a facet of the total school program. Be sure that the job has status attached to it.

3. Invite her and another teacher to accompany you and your family to the theatre or to a special event.

4. Encourage her to join a woman's club in the community.

5. Arrange a surprise birthday party for her.

6. Make her feel wanted and needed by the organization.

2

Problems of

Instructional Techniques

The teaching styles of teachers are almost as varied as the individual differences which exist among members of a staff. Fortunately, most teachers have exemplary interactions with children and follow acceptable teaching modes that promote student growth. Some styles, however, need reshaping, and a few patterns have no place whatsoever in elementary school instruction.

The differences in methodology result from differences in training, experience, and personality. In cases where a particular style has existed for a long period of time, such as the traditional style of teaching, the principal must use slow, indirect, and at times subtle procedures to bring about change. In the case of a recent graduate or some other new teacher, the principal may be more direct. Whatever the case, what is done should be done in a way which will enable the teacher in question to retain his confidence and positive self-concept.

41

Nondirective Teachers

"I have a teacher who gives very little over-all direction to instruction. The children appear to work on their own and are allowed to do almost anything they want to do. A formal learning situation is rare in this room."

Since the last decade there has been increasing interest on the part of researchers in examining the act of teaching. While this particular area of research is young, its findings are bringing about a fresh look at teaching and learning. Recent studies have been concerned with the verbal behavior patterns of teachers which are direct and indirect or dominative and democratic. Some researchers assume that verbal behavior is indicative of total behavior. A few studies show that achievement is higher and that more desirable attitudes are fostered when children are exposed to indirect teaching patterns. Indirect teaching is characterized by acceptance of students' feelings and ideas and by the use of praise and questions. Direct teaching patterns, which include lectures, directions, and individual criticism, contribute to lower achivement and encourage undesirable attitudes.

In our own day as a result of research on child growth and development, flexible desks and chairs in the classroom have replaced bolted-down furniture, and democratic instruction has supplanted the regimentation of early education. The old time education which was good for our fathers is clearly not good enough for us.

Some excellent teachers who use the indirect method are often improperly classified as laissez-faire or nondirective teachers. Occasionally an indirect teacher may lean too far, but even at that, his leaning is usually in the right direction. You don't want to attempt to structure the indirect teacher very much. It seems that a variety of acceptable teacher types is good for a school and better yet for children.

If the teacher in question is truly a laissez-faire teacher and not an indirect teacher, then some kind of action may be necessary. Research studies show that children drift aimlessly and learn very little when direction and control of a learning situation are continually absent to a large degree. This being so, it is imperative that definite steps be taken. To correct or prevent such practices a weekly grade level planning session is suggested, since this encourages the structuralization of content and lesson format. Each Friday teachers can be required to submit to the principal a brief list of the specific items which they will teach the following week. This list, attached to plan books which are submitted to the office on Friday afternoon, also will help to crystallize teaching. Suggest that only book page numbers for the various subjects or content areas appear in the plan book. See Chapter 3 for a discussion of plan books. At the beginning of the school year, each teacher can submit on a 3 × 5 index card a weekly schedule of the approximate hours of the school day the various subjects will be taught. It is the job of the principal to see that each teacher plans his work and works his plan. Good planning on the part of teachers and adequate supervision of classroom activities by the principal have a salutary effect on the entire instructional program. While the principalship was established for the main purpose of overseeing instruction, too often many principals observe individual classrooms no more than once or twice during the school year.

Suggested Guidelines:

1. Recognize that indirective teaching, often confused with laissez-faire or nondirective teaching, offers benefits to learning such as higher achievement and the development of more desirable attitudes.

2. Encourage the teacher to develop, within the framework of his personality and interests, an instructional technique recognized and supported by the best findings of research.

3. Recognize the benefits that different but acceptable teaching styles can offer education.

4. Request from each teacher at the beginning of the school year a 3 × 5 index card indicating a weekly schedule of subjects or subject areas.

5. Require weekly grade-level planning sessions. Convince the staff of the need for and importance of the sessions.

6. Require teachers to submit each Friday a list of teaching goals for the succeeding week to the principal.

7. Require that plan books, which are structured according to content areas, be submitted each Friday. However, do not require detailed lesson plans.

8. Conscientiously supervise all classroom instruction.

TRADITIONAL TEACHERS

"One of my teachers gives very little regard to children in her instruction. The children's desks are in straight rows, she lectures a lot, few projects are carried on, teacher-centered activities dominate the program, and the children have little opportunity to interact verbally."

There are some principals who maintain that as long as pupil achievement is high in a traditionally oriented classroom, there exists no significant problem. This is tantamount to supporting any method, even hitting or threatening children, in order to get satisfactory pupil achievement.

Traditional teachers are clearly out of step with acceptable practice when research findings of child growth and development are considered. But a principal must acknowledge that a traditional teacher has many fine attributes, such as excellent routines, good discipline, definite content, and parental appreciation of his efforts. These teachers often possess many of the characteristics which are only acquired by experience.

An attempt should be made to have them consider the characteristitics of children in their teaching. But go slowly. A teaching pattern that was poured twenty years ago and allowed to set is going to be impervious to almost any change, particularly any attempt of a direct nature. This problem of changing traditional teachers is a testy one. We want to encourage, not embarrass. We want teachers to feel confident, not insecure. We want teachers to be happy, not frightened. We want a teacher's self-concept to grow, not to deteriorate.

These teachers need opportunities to catch up with the advances in education. Whatever is done should be done indirectly. Have a teachers' bulletin board display magazine and newspaper pictures and clippings about special educational projects. Encourage traditional teachers to enroll in graduate work, ostensibly to get pay raises. If enough teachers are interested in taking a course, call the university officials and ask them if they can schedule a course at your school.

A year's free subscription to *Grade Teacher* or *The Instructor* will help to expose the traditional teacher to many stimuli on acceptable contemporary teaching; inroads will be made. Hire young promising graduates who follow the latest methods of teaching and hopefully some of their methods will rub off on the traditional teacher. When demonstrations are held or when teachers are encouraged to combine their classes occasionally for instruction or for culminating activities in social studies units, teachers learn new techniques and ideas from each other. Schedule group discussions at which newer and more acceptable teaching practices are examined. Bi-weekly grade level meetings can be held during which teachers share and plan a unit of work together.

Each school staff should meet at least two times each year to discuss new approaches, developments, and research in the field. The discussion may cover such topics as the new math (*e.g.*, SMSG materials), guidance counselors in elementary schools, team or large group teaching, ungraded organization plans, what research says about diagramming sentences and teaching grammar, and Initial Teaching Alphabet (i/t/a), or the new approach to reading. Much of the reasoning for or against new developments is based on a consideration of the characteristics of children. When teachers consider children in their instruction, traditionalism begins to break down.

When the occasion presents itself, praise a teacher—one whom the traditional teacher admires—for giving consideration to the development of children in some part of her teaching. It may be a subtle remark or an innocent comment, such as, "I like the arrangement of your desks. It's much more attractive than straight rows, and provides for better social development." For some teachers a hint is sufficient to effectuate change. Praise the traditional teacher for any manifestation of change toward acceptable new methods. Tell her why you have complimented her. This will reinforce the change which has been made. Use indirect methods in attempting to bring about change. This traditional teacher has probably given faithful service for a number of years. Her strong assets contribute significantly to the staff. Be kind and consider her feelings. Above all, don't expect change overnight.

Suggested Guidelines:

1. Use indirect methods to bring about change.

2. Build on her strong assets; don't tear her down by pointing up her weaknesses.

3. In her presence, praise a teacher whom she admires for some evidence of good teaching.

4. Provide current materials, books, magazines, and displays on education.

5. Attempt to get a university to hold courses in your school district.

6. Hold regular grade level meetings for planning and sharing.

7. Conduct symposiums and discussions on new concepts and practices for elementary education.

8. Praise the traditional teacher for any evidence of change, and state the rationale supporting the change.

9. Hire promising young graduates schooled in fresh, new approaches.

10. Encourage teachers to combine classes for instructional periods and culminating activities.

TEACHERS FROM SECONDARY SCHOOL

"This year a junior high school teacher was transferred to my school. What can I do to help her adjust to this level of teaching?"

A person who has been trained for one level of instruction and, for some reason or another is required to work on another, needs a broad sense of confidence. Teaching on the secondary level and teaching on the elementary level are disparate functions. The former entails content, and the latter involves a fusion of skills and knowledge about content and children. The principal's first step is to make known to the teacher his confidence and faith in her. Tell her you recognize and respect the knowledge in a specialized subject field which she has.

Next, until the teacher gets some experience in elementary school instruction, it is wise to assign her to an upper elementary grade since the differences here will not be as great as with a primary group. Also, ask a veteran teacher, one on her same grade level if possible, to be her "buddy." This will provide strong support for the new teacher during the difficult first year.

Observing competent teachers in the classroom is imperative for this teacher. While regular teachers rarely observe other teachers, to do so is one of the most effective ways of up-grading and improving instruction. During the first month of school make three or four appointments for the new teacher to observe other teachers in your own or nearby schools. As the principal, you should accompany the teacher so you can discuss the observed classroom methods and procedures and explain the rationale supporting them.

A year's free subscription to *Grade Teacher* or *The Instructor* is helpful. Use the petty cash fund to do this. Lend books, journals, or monographs dealing with child growth and development. The school should have a subscription to some scholarly journals. The topic of child growth and development often needs reviewing by all teachers; therefore, the transplanted secondary school teacher could be a member of a faculty committee which will lead a faculty group discussion on the subject.

Encourage the teacher to take at least one course a semester at a nearby college if possible. The teacher has the advantage of immediately putting into practice during the day what she has learned in the evening.

During the first year the teacher is closely supervised so that a strong foundation in elementary teaching will be established. Praise her when you observe that she considers the characteristics of children in her teaching. Don't expect results over-night. Be patient. For most teachers, the art of teaching children is developed over the years.

Suggested Guidelines:

1. Express confidence and faith in the content contribution the teacher will make.

2. Assign the teacher to an upper elementary grade.

3. Ask a competent teacher to be her "Buddy."

4. Have the teacher observe competent teachers in action. Ac-

company her on teacher-observation assignments so that she gains meaning and understanding.

5. Give the teacher a year's free subscription to *Grade Teacher* or *The Instructor*.

6. Lend books, journals, or monographs dealing with child growth and development.

7. Schedule in-service meetings to discuss the characteristics of children and their relationship to teaching.

8. Supervise the teacher closely and have frequent follow-up conferences.

9. Praise the teacher upon evidence of growth.

10. Encourage the teacher to take evening education courses at a university. The selected courses should contribute directly to teaching.

NEW TEACHERS

"What can I do to make sure potential staff members will fit smoothly into the school's educative program?"

It usually takes a principal a number of years to get a school operating in a way which is acceptable both to him and to his teachers. It takes some principals longer than others. While change for improvement is one thing, change sponsored by a rebellious new member can wreak havoc upon a smoothly operating school. The key to the solution of the problem lies in the recruiting process.

There are several ways by which a principal may smoothly merge a new teacher into an established organization. First, each teacher candidate should be observed teaching in a classroom; this includes student teachers. Some contend that a teacher always performs better when an observer is in the room. This is probably true but, in some instances, a teacher's best may not be good enough for your school.

If you decide, on the basis of this observation, that the teacher appears promising, you can then make an appointment for a personal interview with him at your school. At this time an application for employment can be completed. The personal interview is the most effective method of obtaining information about the candidate and assessing his potentialities. Don't talk in generalities; tell the teacher candidate specifically about your school: its philosophy, curriculum offerings, how class enrollments are determined, special duties of teachers, building routines, night meetings, and salary increments. Find out if any of his ideas or opinions are sharply opposed to your school program. Make sure he likes children and enjoys being around them. Find out if he has worked with children in his leisure time or during the summer months. Include a tour of the building and the school district. Give him a copy of the teachers' handbook to take with him.

If you are impressed by the interview, follow up your personal evaluation by sending for the candidate's credentials (you may already have them) from the college or commercial placement bureau. After the credentials are examined, check the references and past employers, preferably by telephone. Employers are less willing to put negative evaluations in writing than to discuss them over the telephone. This check with references and past employers should be done for *all* candidates, even if the candidate appears to be a Montessori. The check with persons who have known or supervised the candidate will provide invaluable data on the candidate's past work history. A record of the candidate's previous performance is the best single index of how he can be expected to work in a future position. When you contact the references by telephone, include a check-off list of questions: teaching ability; sick leave taken; relations with children, colleagues, parents; and cooperation with administrators. A word of caution, however, is important: if a past principal speaks with disfavor about the potential teacher, be sure to weigh the evaluations of all authorities carefully. You may have under consideration an excellent teacher who at one time had the misfortune to work in a school with a poor principal.

Suggested Guidelines:

1. Observe the teacher candidate in action in the classroom.

2. Be specific in the personal interview. Find out if any of his ideas are in conflict with the guiding principles of your school program.

3. Examine closely the applicant's credentials to determine the length of time a job was held and the reasons for leaving positions. Also, find out about *unexplained* time between positions.

4. Use the telephone to check references and past employers of all prospective employees.

YOUNG GRADUATES

"What can I do to help young graduates during their first year in teaching?"

This is probably the first full-time professional position for most of the young graduates. Their first experience and impression must be rewarding and positive if they are to remain in the field of education.

In the beginning of the school year, teachers usually report to their schools a few days before the children arrive. Many principals introduce the young graduates at the pre-school faculty meeting, but some principals do little beyond this. On the first day the young graduate reports to the school take him to his classroom. Do not tell him it is Room 6 and expect him to find it; go with him. Introduce him to the non-professional staff and the teachers adjacent to his classroom.

If you have several young graduates or new teachers, you will want to meet with them as a group to reiterate some of the school policies you mentioned when they were interviewed for the job. Getting them together in a group will reduce their anxieties because they will realize there are other new teachers in the same situation they are in. Avoid overburdening them with policy facts. They won't remember most of what you say. Tell them about the things which will immediately affect them: the school day hours for teachers and pupils, the lunch times and lunch costs, parking for teachers, and outside areas of play for their classes. Introduce the new teacher to a regular member of the staff, a friendly person who is near his age and who will be his *buddy* for the first year.

After this, first day policies vary according to the different principals. Some principals give very little direction; others supervise the neophyte very closely. Principals have a responsibility for helping the new teacher, but too much direction will hinder rather than help development. During the first few weeks you may want to let a young graduate operate with minimal supervision. This will enable classroom routines to be established; also, it will give the teacher a chance to learn the "lay of the land" and to discover and define a few areas in which help is needed.

Some regularly scheduled plan for assisting the beginner should start sometime within the last two weeks of September. Some principals use pre-observation conferences in which the teacher and principal go over the lesson plan that will be used when the principal makes an observation. Other principals schedule one weekly visit of two hours. If appropriate, during the visit the principal should help the teacher; he should not sit like a judge in the rear of the room. A brief conference, if needed, can be held in the classroom immediately after the visit. Ideally, the conference should be held in the teacher's classroom after school when the children have left. Avoid telling the teacher what could be done to improve instruction. Make suggestions and give the rationale which supports each suggestion. Reinforce the things he did well with favorable comments. Refrain from doing all or most of the talking. If you fail to do this, there will be no significant feedback from the teacher. Elicit suggestions for improvement from the teacher himself. At the conclusion of the conference summarize the discussion. Keep a written record of each conference and provide written suggestions for the teacher. Follow up these suggestions on the next visit.

A regular weekly appointment for classroom visitation should be made for the first four or five months. This will provide enough time for the teacher to develop confidence in you and in his teaching. Sometime during the second half of the school year, some unannounced biweekly visits can be made.

Young graduates bring spontaneity and enthusiasm to their first job. Some doubts are raised in their minds, however, when principals and veteran teachers tell them, "You'll go by the book in the beginning, but you'll change! You'll change!" Be positive and encourage their efforts. Be patient and assist them.

Suggested Guidelines:

1. Develop a definite orientation program for all new teachers.

2. Use the "buddy system" for young graduates and other new teachers.

3. Let the young graduate learn the "lay of the land" his first month on the job.

4. Schedule a weekly visitation to the teacher:

    a. Use the visit to help the teacher, not to watch him.
    b. Have conferences in the teacher's classroom on the same day of the visit.
    c. Give the teacher a written summary of the conference.
    d. Follow-up written suggestions.

5. Build upon the strength of the new teacher. Lend positive support. Give a generous portion of praise when it is deserved.

TEACHERS WITH NO TRAINING IN EDUCATION

"The superintendent assigned a liberal arts graduate to my school. He has never had a course in education. Where do I start?"

Surveys show that a liberal arts graduate is at a disadvantage in almost any specialized area of work during the first years, but after this, he soon catches up and in many cases overtakes his specialized colleagues. The problem presented by the liberal arts graduate on the staff is comparable to the one presented by the converted secondary school teacher. A large proportion of the graduates of liberal arts colleges have a concentration in a subject field which qualifies them to teach only on the secondary level. For suggested guidelines, refer to the topic entitled "Teachers From Secondary School."

3

Curricular

Problems

A principal's duties can usually be separated into two broad categories: business and curriculum. Although the administrator invariably spends a disproportionate amount of his time with the *business* of running a school, few would debate the paramount importance of the *curriculum*. It is the curriculum which provides the framework upon which the teaching-learning act is dependent. Stone, mortar, teachers, and instructional materials have been brought together for only one purpose—to teach children! It is, therefore, an understatement to say that the problems of the curriculum are among the most serious facing the principal. In many of these problems, the teacher is involved, for curriculum problems and teacher-personnel problems are often closely intertwined. And yet many of the problems of personnel are very closely related to the area of curriculum.

In the broad definition of the word, curriculum includes all the experiences a child has under the aegis of the school. In a stricter sense of the word, curriculum, as used in this chapter, entails those activities which are for the most part related to an individual teacher's classroom instructional program.

CLASSROOM CLIMATE

"It seems that classroom climate has an effect on a host of things. Is there any way to improve the climate of a room?"

Classroom climate, researchers tell us, is determined more by the verbal behavior of a teacher than by any other factor. The assumption that researchers make is that the pattern of verbal behavior—dominative (direct) or democratic (indirect)—is indicative of total behavior. Dominative verbal behavior is characterized by the use of lecture, the giving directions or commands, and continual criticism. Verbal behavior of a democratic nature encompasses accepting children's feelings, giving praise and encouragement, accepting and restating children's ideas, and asking questions. The general verbal pattern of a teacher is the pattern which children adopt. Democratic patterns beget democratic patterns; dominative patterns lead only to further domination.

Researchers are careful to advocate the use of both dominative and democratic patterns, according to the instances which occur in the classroom; but their findings from experimental studies stress that when the pattern of a teacher's verbal interaction with children is generally democratic, pupil achievement is higher, and desirable attitudes are fostered. On the other hand, when a teacher constantly uses a dominative pattern of verbal interaction, achievement is lower and less desirable attitudes are formed.

There are various verbal interaction systems. The Minnesota Categories system has been termed the most reliable device yet developed, and is being used in in-service workshops at the University of Minnesota, University of Michigan, and Temple University. This system can be easily learned by a classroom teacher and used to improve his verbal behavior. The booklet *The Role of the Teacher in the Classroom, A Manual for Understanding and Improving Teachers' Classroom Behavior*, by Edmund Amidon and Ned Flanders, describes the system and can be obtained for

$1.50 from Paul S. Amidon & Associates, Inc., 429–432 Plymouth Bldg., Minneapolis 31, Minnesota.

Suggested Guidelines:

1. Recognize that the verbal behavior of a teacher affects classroom climate more than any other factor.

2. The suggested verbal interaction system is the Minnesota Categories. Teachers can easily learn the system, code their verbal behavior from magnetic tapes, and attempt to change or improve their verbal communication with children.

ABILITY GROUPING

"My teachers complain that teaching a heterogeneous class is difficult. They want to change to homogeneous classes."

Unless there are enough children so very high or so very low in intelligence as to warrant homogeneous classes, the best education, I firmly believe, is gotten by interactions of pupils with other pupils of dissimilar backgrounds, experiences, and socio-economic and intelligence levels. Where the "track" system, or homogeneous grouping, is practiced, children and children's parents are often unfairly discriminated against. The children in the upper track and their parents are looked up to; the boys and girls in the low track and their parents are looked down at.

Suggested Guidelines:

1. Consider and weigh carefully the advantages and disadvantages which any form of school organization offers.

2. Homogeneous grouping has serious short-comings which threaten not only the children in the lower and upper groups but also their parents.

GROUPING VS. NON-GROUPING IN CLASSROOMS

"Within the classroom, I think teachers should group the children in some subjects according to ability and achievement. Some teachers have resisted my efforts to get them to group."

For some teachers, grouping within the classroom is a difficult form of organization to manage. Frequently, educational literature refers to grouping as a "three ring circus." The management skills and abilities of some teachers are suited to grouping; primary teachers seem to excel at it. This is a procedure which I leave to each teacher, for even the educational experts disagree on grouping within a classroom for the various subjects. Although grouping provides for individual differences, there are some very real and obvious disadvantages in using grouping—disadvantages to both teacher and pupils.

If some teachers show a willingness to try it, you can have them observe a few teachers in the school who successfully practice grouping. At the beginning the teacher can group only a few times a week. The first week or two you can help the teacher. Gradually taper off your assistance. Develop guidelines for grouping with the teacher. For instance, it is essential that the group which is working without the teacher knows precisely what they are to do. If they don't, they will interrupt the teacher with questions. Appointing a student leader for the teacherless group will go far in enabling the teacher to work uninterruptedly with the other group; also, the student leader will get valuable leadership experience. The teacher should divide her time evenly between the groups. Often, the top group is neglected by the teacher, but they also need teacher guidance.

Informal, flexible groupings based on the immediate common problems and needs of certain children should be used by every teacher. For example, organize groups for five or six children who need help with the use of the comma; three children who need special help with a two place multiplier; two children who frequently misspell the same simple words. These informal groups can meet for a brief period of time, from five to fifteen minutes. No child feels inferior because he is in such a group, because he knows all members of the class will be in a similar group at one time or another during the school year.

Suggested Guidelines:

1. Encourage, but don't demand, intra-class grouping. There are some teachers who are unsuccessful with grouping, and want no part of it. The production of these teachers will be higher without the use of groups.

2. Help the teacher who is willing to try grouping.

   a. Have the teacher observe teachers who use grouping successfully.
   b. Develop with the teacher some guidelines for grouping.
   c. Suggest that the teacher try grouping only a couple of times a week until confidence is developed.
   d. Assist the teacher when she initially tries grouping; gradually taper off your help.

3. Persuade teachers to use small, flexible, informal groups to reteach units or work with common problems.

PLAN BOOKS

"Should principals require teachers to prepare detailed lesson plans?"

How lesson plans are handled by the principal depends to a large extent on the kind of staff he has. If the staff has a record of successful teaching, I suggest that the preparation of lesson plans be made optional, except as noted below. For an inexperienced teacher, however, lesson plans provide the structure needed for lessons.

I know a principal who, early each school year, obtains a file folder from each teacher which has pertinent information for the use of the substitute teacher. Such information includes recess and lunch times; which playground to use; supervisory schedules and duties; the schedules of art, music, physical education and foreign languages; and information about certain children with specific problems. These file folders are kept in the secretary's office and are given to the substitute teacher when she arrives. When a teacher has to be absent, he submits to the office a brief lesson plan which will be placed in his folder. If an occasional emergency occurs and the teacher is unexpectedly absent, the principal briefs the substitute teacher. This plan works well because the teachers will honor the requirement of submitting a lesson plan the day before they are going to be absent. Also, the folder adds important supplemental data.

There is another principal I know who had his teachers submit lesson plans only when they were going to be absent. However, his teachers were negligent even under this generous arrangement. So he now has them submit, each Friday, the lesson plans for the following week. He only requires page numbers for the various subject areas, or a brief description of the activities which are planned.

Still another principal requires that brief weekly lesson plans be kept in the middle drawer of the teacher's desk. He rarely checks lesson plan books, but, at the end of the day, each substitute teacher fills out a brief questionnaire which is turned in to the office. The questions cover completeness of lesson plans, behavior and attitudes of pupils, and any specific problems encountered. Also, space is provided for negative and positive comments. The teachers know about this questionnaire, and the plan operates smoothly.

Choose the system which fits your situation. But do not require teachers to prepare the kind of lesson plans which are required of student teachers. Planning a day's work is imperative, but detailed lesson plans are not necessary. Experienced teachers seldom use them. Teachers have many other more profitable ways of spending their time than spelling out the details that their skill and experience will dictate as they go along.

Suggested Guidelines:

1. Select the plan which fits your situation:

   a. Have each teacher submit to the office a file folder with pertinent information about schedules, duties, recess and lunch times, and certain problem children. The teacher also submits a lesson plan the day before his absence.

   b. Require teachers to turn in lesson plans for the following week each Friday.

   c. Require that weekly lesson plans be kept in the teachers' desks.

2. Suggest that teachers prepare only brief, skeletal lesson plans, no matter which plan is used.

3. Include some kind of evaluative design to be used by the substitute teacher.

PLANNING TIME

"My teachers have requested that they be given some time each week for planning instruction. They have suggested that the pupils be dismissed an hour earlier each Thursday so that grade level meetings can be held."

I think it is commendable that your teachers have asked for planning time. I know a few principals who would flatly deny this request and tell the teachers to hold grade level meetings after school. It is these principals who think teachers should stay at work daily from thirty minutes to an hour after a teacher's day is officially over. They fail to recognize the extra hours teachers put in at their homes correcting papers, planning the next day's work, and so forth. And they forget that many of the teachers are wives and mothers who have dinners to prepare.

You will have to consider your state law which gives the minimum number of hours that children are required to be in school. If you have an extra school hour for each week, you could dismiss school an hour early each Thursday. If you have two extra hours, school could be dismissed at noon one day a week. If your school hours for pupils are just meeting the state law requirement, lengthening the school day by an adjustment of fifteen minutes in the beginning or closing of school would permit school to close an hour earlier one day a week. If the school day cannot be lengthened, the lunch hour, if it is extra long, could be trimmed by fifteen minutes. Don't trim a forty-five minute lunch hour though. The children need about twenty minutes to eat lunch and another twenty minutes to be what they are: children that need to romp, play, and relax.

Suggested Guidelines:

1. Teachers who request planning time have imagination and initiative. They'll make good use of the time.

2. Find out how many school pupil-hours are required by state law.

3. If you are marginally meeting the state law requirement, increase the school day by fifteen minutes at the beginning or end of the school day, or trim a long lunch hour. This will give an extra hour a week.

4. Consider the effects on the children before making any adjustments.

Marking System

"My teachers have different criteria for the achievement marks they give pupils. Some mark on the 100 point system, others give marks on the basis of how a pupil compares with his class, and still other teachers give a child a mark based on whether he is working up to his ability. Should a marking standard be established for all the teachers of the school?"

Yes, I think a school staff should agree on an interpretation of the academic mark; in other words, they should agree on what "the mark means," not "the method" of arriving at the mark. Even when a marking standard is established and defined, it is still difficult to explain what an A, B, C, or any mark really means. An anecdotal type of report card seems to be the best kind of written reporting device. However, parents are traditionally oriented to a marking system based on letters. They want to know where their child is on the lettered continuum; therefore, the alphabetical marking system remains with us. Some school staffs have developed a marking system which accounts for a pupil's relative standing in the class and his achievement in relation to his ability. An example is the mark of B_1. The B indicates that the pupil is doing above average work in relation to his class. The subscript$_1$ denotes that he is working on his ability level. Another possible mark is B_2. The B means the same as before, but the subscript indicates the pupil is working below his ability level. Other refinements could be added. To have a reliable marking system, each teacher should use a marking book together with some kind of anecdotal record, or a folder with written evidence of a pupil's work.

Although it is desirable that a marking system have lucid definitions, the method by which a teacher arrives at the mark, I believe, is the teacher's prerogative. Some teachers mark on a curve; others assign marks on a 100 maximum point system; some assign a report card mark from various combinations of marks, for example, 30% of the mark from classroom work, 50% from examinations, and 20% from homework. To dictate or to establish by consensus the method of determining a mark, it seems, is an infringement of a teacher's right to decide his own method.

Suggested Guidelines:

1. Strive for parent and teacher acceptance of a report card which provides for teachers' evaluative comments for the subject areas.

2. Standardize with the help of the staff a marking system for the school. Provide refinements that tell a parent how Tommy's achievement compares with that of members of his class and with his own potentiality.

3. Permit teacher autonomy in determining the method to be used in assigning marks.

4. Encourage the use of a marking book and folders containing samples of written work.

STANDARDIZED TESTING PROGRAM

"Most of my teachers do not use the standardized testing program properly. They correct the tests, record the scores in the cumulative records, and leave them there, for the most part—seldom if ever using them."

A school is considered behind the times if it does not have a standardized testing program. A few teachers make good use of the tests. Unfortunately, there are some teachers who never give the test results a second glance once they are filed away. Now why is this? It is probably because teachers do not know how to use the tool. One cannot use a tool which he does not fully understand how to use. The tools that help us the most are the tools we understand.

If you doubt this, ask your staff at the next faculty meeting if anyone knows the difference between a mean, median, and mode. These simple measures of central tendency can tell a teacher how to adapt her instruction to the class. What is urgently needed in many teachers' colleges is instruction in methods of using test results in teaching—the diagnostic and evaluative uses. If you are in a county system, request a speaker from the county testing office. If you are principal of a small school district, share a university consultant with your neighboring districts. Have the topic treated in a simple and practicable manner, and have the speaker discuss only what teachers can use.

A principal should know how his school ranks with national norms. Have the teachers submit class means. If two tests are given on a grade level, you want the teachers to plot a scattergram which correlates these two scores.* Underachievers and overachievers would be graphically illustrated if one test were an intelligence test. Your consultant can suggest other ways in which test scores have value to teachers.

Suggested Guidelines:

1. If you have spent money on a testing program, make sure the teachers know how to use test results.

2. Arrange for a consultant from the county office or a nearby college to acquaint teachers with diagnostic and evaluative uses of tests.

3. Whatever you request teachers to do with test scores, be sure that it has direct applicability to their teaching.

CUMULATIVE RECORDS

"*Some of my teachers do a poor job with children's cumulative records. Some records are inadequately filled out and other records are not even kept.*"

Some records are necessary, but many others are not. Half the contents

---

*If two different test populations were used to build the norms, caution should be used in relating the results of the two tests.

of some cumulative records could be discarded without harm. The first step is to determine which records should be included and which records do not help teachers. Since the teachers use the records more than anybody else, they should have a major voice in these decisions.

List the records which are required for each cumulative folder. Hand out this list in September with implicit instructions on filling out the records. Set a date early in the school year—about November 1st—when all cumulative records must be turned in for inspection. If an inspection is not conducted early in the school year, the records of some children will not be completed until May or June. If this happens, the incomplete records will be of little assistance to the teacher during the school year, and a child transferring out of the school may have incomplete records mailed to his new school. Since a principal rarely has time to inspect each child's cumulative record, select at random a half dozen records for inspection from each classroom.

Because additional information for records is accumulated during the school year, make another random inspection during May. Be sure to announce the inspection date well in advance so teachers will have their records completed.

Suggested Guidelines:

1. Determine with the staff's help the records which will be kept for the children.

2. In September, distribute to the teachers a list of the required records; include clear explanations for completing the records.

3. Inspect the cumulative records both early and late in the school year; set inspection dates well in advance so teachers will have time to complete the records.

CONTROVERSIAL TEACHING METHODS

"Occasionally a teacher will work on a special class project which other teachers think is a waste of time. How can these controversial teaching methods be handled by the principal?"

All special classroom projects of any size should be cleared through the principal's office. A principal should ascertain whether the goals of the project are worthwhile in relation to the time it will take to accomplish them. Teachers will be inclined to take a positive attitude toward a questionable project when they know the principal has approved it. The instructional benefits of an activity should be mentioned in a faculty meeting or in the staff newsletter. This provides information of an in-service nature as well as an incentive for other teachers to engage in interesting class activities.

Sterile, stereotyped teaching will occur less frequently if teachers know they have administrative support to try new approaches and to risk taking chances. Often we think of individual differences in a negative way. But the factor of individual differences is more positive than negative. Different ideas should be encouraged, and teachers should be urged to develop better methods. Whether or not there will be creativity in teaching is often determined more by the principal's attitude than by the teachers' talents.

Suggested Guidelines:

1. All special activities and projects should be approved by the principal.

2. An approved project is of interest and benefit to the staff. Mention it in a faculty meeting, give the learning goals.

3. Promote a school climate which stimulates and inspires creativity in instruction.

OMITTED SCIENCE PROGRAMS

"In our school science is taught as a separate subject. A few of the teachers often neglect teaching it."

I am happy that it is taught as a separate subject because science is important for many reasons: (a) it's all around us; (b) children have need of it in their daily experiences; and (c) they are highly interested in science. Arithmetic and social studies are also concerned with science. A good science program must be consonant with the way children learn—manipulating, discovering, experimenting, doing.

Now why do teachers shy away from teaching science? It is not because they don't like it, for they teach the other basic subjects, whether they like them or not. This question is easily answered. In the first place, science is different; but the *basic* reason is that many teachers have not studied science themselves. Many have but a few science courses on their transcripts. Not just the college transcript, but the secondary school transcript as well; and not just *these* transcripts, but the elementary school transcript too. You see, the addition of science as a subject important enough to be put into the curriculum in the elementary school on its own merits was made in most school districts during the early fifties, or following "Sputnik." In some prominent school districts science continues to be alternated with social studies. Many teachers have little or no background to teach it. For these teachers, science evokes negative images: chemicals being mixed together with the wrong chemicals causing shattering explosions, things burning, smoke and foul odors in the classroom, complex relationships and unpredictable results, pupils asking perplexing questions, and teachers having to confess "I don't know." And above all, pupils correcting the teacher—an unhappy situation, to say the least.

Therefore, we have to help teachers. We just cannot put the subject of science in the curriculum and tell the teachers to teach it. What if the superintendent tells all the principals that cybernetics is so important for the teaching-learning act, and that each principal must instruct his teachers in its rudiments. After this pronouncement, he gives you a book on the subject. Now this example is not absurd—I had to look up the definition myself after reading that Russia is using cybernetics with teachers—do you get the point?

The teachers need *help*: workshops, consultants, books, monographs, science courses (Content and Method), demonstrations, materials, science kits, films, and instruction in the use of simple materials (including even milk cartons). Some of the publishing companies have science representatives who will conduct workshops for your staff. Universities will be glad to help build a science curriculum. They are happy to provide consultants. If you can get enough teachers, they will even provide a course for credit which can be held at your school.

Plan an occasional science lesson with each teacher. This is one area in which it is going to take time for teachers to both build up a background and be confident in that background.

Suggested Guidelines:

1. Recognize that many teachers have inadequate backgrounds in science.

2. Provide opportunities for teachers to improve themselves: books, monographs, journals, simple materials, workshops, etc.

3. Seek assistance from higher education: consultants, a credit course in science held at your school or in your school district, etc.

4. Assist the teacher as often as you can with science lessons.

5. Send for: *Teaching Elementary Science, Suggestions for Classroom Teachers* (OE-29011) by Glenn O. Blough and Paul E. Blackwood; Superintendent of Documents, U.S. Government Printing Office, Washington 25, D.C. (Price 20¢.)

    For information on science kits and science supplies: Science Kit, Inc., Tonawanda, New York.

AUDIO-VISUALS

"We have audio-visual equipment and materials in our school, but my teachers seldom use them. How can teachers be encouraged to use audio-visual equipment in their instruction?"

Audio-visuals should be correlated to the instructional program of specific classrooms. Except for a few instances in which films are shown simultaneously to several grade levels because of their general educational value, audio-visuals should be used in the classrooms.

Surveys have pointed up the educational value of audio-visual equipment and materials in instruction. If teachers are not using available audio-visual aids, something needs to be done. The first thing is to find out if the teachers know what A-V materials and equipment are available and how these materials can reinforce classroom instruction. Perhaps the teachers do not know how to operate the machines. Many state departments of education now require a course in audio-visuals for teacher certification. Some older teachers have never had any training in the use of A-V materials; others, unfortunately, who have "successfully" passed a course in audio-visuals, still do not feel confident in using the machines. Women tend to rate themselves low in mechanical ability, although there does not appear to be any valid basis for the rating. A workshop designed to acquaint teachers with the equipment would help to solve this problem, but this is not enough.

The A-V program of a school needs a director who will supervise and maintain the program. Often, faulty machines discourage teacher usage. A burned-out bulb, a blown fuse, an inoperative switch, a missing extension cord, a broken record player needle, or no magnetic tape for the tape recorder all point up the need for an able director who will maintain an effective audio-visual program and encourage school-wide use of audio-visual materials.

Another reason why audio-visuals are not used is the inaccessibility of the equipment or materials. An opaque projector will remain in the storage room if a teacher has to carry it up a flight of steps or fifty feet to her classroom. Heavy machines should be on portable carriages; moreover, each floor level should have its own equipment. Also, a filmstrip library should be located in the school. Films will be used more frequently if a teacher does not have to requisition them from a source away from the school.

Suggested Guidelines:

1. Adapt classrooms to A-V equipment.

2. Provide duplicate A-V equipment, such as tape recorders and filmstrip projectors.

3. Schedule in-service workshop meetings with audio-visual equipment and materials.

4. Ensure that A-V materials and equipment are accessible to teachers.

5. Purchase portable carriages for heavy machines.

6. Require teachers to submit a written monthly report of their use of audio-visuals.

7. Appoint an audio-visual aids director whose duties will be to:

   a. Conduct refresher courses in the beginning of each school year in the use of A-V equipment and materials.
   b. Introduce and explain the operation of new equipment and aids.
   c. Inspect machines for defects and send defective machines for repair.
   d. Supervise the ordering, receiving, distribution, and return of rented or borrowed A-V materials.

RESOURCE SPEAKERS

"I encourage teachers to use resource people in the classroom because this is a good way to add enrichment to learning, but rarely do my teachers use resource people."

Using resource people is one of the most inexpensive and yet effective ways of providing enrichment. If teachers knew which people were available, special speakers would be used more. And, if you just look around, you'll find diamonds in your own backyard. What about the non-professional staff at the school? One teacher I know has the school secretary, the cook, the bus driver, and the custodian speak to the class about their jobs. Some of the mysteries surrounding these people, whom the children see every day, are unveiled. The children get a peek behind the scenes, and they suddenly begin to appreciate these people. In the future they will be more willing to help them.

There is another teacher who, early in the school year, sends home a letter to the parents inviting them to share their hobbies, special interests, travel experiences, or talents with the class. Each parent indicates whether or not he is willing to speak to the class some time during the school year, and returns the form to the teacher. This teacher has had very interesting and varied talks by parents—ranging from a talk on lifesaving to a demonstration of electronics.

Clergymen also have much to offer. In the first place, they are accustomed to speaking before children and adults; and, they usually have some interesting avocations. Veterans are another good source, especially those who have some travel experience. Pupils whose fathers, uncles, and other relatives have been in the military service can make the arrangements for you. Another teacher invites each father to speak to the class about his job. What an excellent source for vocational guidance!

One principal I know has a file of available speakers for teachers from the town's service clubs and other local organizations. He wrote to each club and solicited available speakers. He keeps the list current by contacting the clubs every couple of years.

The principal should have control over who is to speak and the topic of the talk. State in the teachers' handbook that all resource people are to be cleared by you.

Suggested Guidelines:

1. Encourage the use of resource people.

2. Develop a list of available resource people, together with their topics, addresses, and phone numbers. Make the list available to the staff.

3. Resource possibilities: non-professional staff at the school, parents, clergymen, veterans, representatives or members of service clubs, and employees of various departments of local government.

4. All resource people and their topics should be cleared by the principal.

5. If possible, the principal should attend the special classroom program.

6. Publicize the talk in the local newspaper. Nearly all of the talks are gratis. Recognition, however, does not cost anything in the local newspaper, and it tells the public something about the schools.

SPECIAL ENRICHMENT TEACHERS

"Some of my teachers stay in the classroom with the art and foreign language teachers, or remain with the class for music and physical education. Other teachers go to the teachers' lounge. Should I require teachers to stay with their classes during these times?"

The assumption that was made when these special enrichment teachers were employed was that the classroom teacher was not so well prepared as the special teachers in these particular areas. When a teacher stays with the class, the advantage is that she learns about the use of techniques and materials and becomes aware of what the children are doing, and thus can follow up or supervise some activities after the enrichment teacher leaves. How capable a teacher is to follow up the activities, and whether the special teacher would want it done, are unanswered questions.

If special enrichment teachers were hired because the classroom teacher could not do an acceptable job, of what benefit is it to have a teacher remain with the class? The most important reason *against* teachers staying with their classes is that too many cooks in a kitchen seldom produce results. Who is really in control, the regular teacher or the special teacher? What if both think they are in control?

I request that teachers stay five minutes in the beginning of the art or music period, and return five minutes before the class ends. This procedure affords a smooth transition of the class from one teacher to another, and it gives the two teachers a chance to discuss any problems or special circumstances that warrant consideration.

Suggested Guidelines:

1. When a teacher remains with the special teacher, the disadvantages appear to outweigh the advantages.

2. Request that classroom teachers be with their classes during the first and last five minutes of the special period.

SUBSTITUTE TEACHERS

"Some substitute teachers present problems in our school. They don't do much except baby-sit with the children. Only a few work out very well."

The plan for dealing with substitute teachers is important. Add up the total days that substitute teachers were used in the school year and you'll agree. The principal has certain responsibilities, and among them is his duty to set the responsibilities of both the classroom teacher and the substitute teacher. The staff can help develop these lists of duties.

The regular teacher should leave a schedule of subjects (See PLAN BOOKS in this chapter), her special duties, a copy of the teachers' handbook, and any necessary administrative forms, *e.g.* lunch reports. The names of student leaders in the class should be jotted down. They can help the substitute a great deal. Paper and other needed supplies should be in the room. If there is a special problem pupil in the class, a brief note should be left with instructions on how to handle the child.

The responsibilities of the substitute teacher include adhering to the plans which the regular teacher has left, correcting the work accomplished that day, leaving a record of what was done, and completing and turning in to the office the evaluation form for the benefit of the principal.

The principal should greet the substitute teacher when she arrives and accompany her to the classroom. If the substitute is new, the principal familiarizes her with the cafeteria, the assigned playground, and any pertinent operating procedures. The adjacent classroom teacher should be introduced to the substitute teacher as a helping teacher during the day.

One principal I know conducts a half-day workshop every other summer for substitute teachers. He gives them an overview of the school system policies and his own school policies. He explains the topics in the teachers' handbook. Each substitute receives a handbook to keep. There is a discussion of what is expected of the principal, the teachers, and the substitute teachers. They take a tour of the school. Substitute teachers are more than baby-sitters; instruction of the curriculum must go on. It will go on when sufficient planning is made.

Suggested Guidelines:

1. Conduct a half-day workshop in the summer for substitute teachers. Familiarize them with the school plant, building routines, and operating procedures.

2. List with the staff's help the guidelines which the principal, teachers, and substitute teachers should follow. Here are some suggestions:

    a. Principal's responsibility: greet substitute teacher, accompany her to room, familiarize her with cafeteria, playground, and school routines; introduce her to regular teacher near her classroom.

b. Teachers' responsibility: leave schedule of subjects, list of duties, teachers' handbook, administrative forms, necessary supplies, names of student helpers, and instructions for dealing with special problem pupils.

c. Substitute teacher's responsibility: follow plans of regular teacher, correct work accomplished that day, leave report of work done, and complete and turn in to the office the evaluation form.

GUIDANCE

"My teachers say they don't have time to give attention to the personal guidance of pupils."

I once heard a venerated educator refer to the guidance program in the elementary school as a red herring. Whether he was right or not, on this topic I seem to voice the sentiments of many teachers who say the basic subjects keep them busy enough. One of the basic requirement of a good guidance program is that it serve all the students. This is a fairly large task. When I was a classroom teacher I was almost out of gas at the end of the day, and when I added a guidance program, I was empty before the last bell rang. But elementary school students need personal guidance. Some, of course, need it more than others. When a child needs help, whether with the curricular content or with personal problems, every possible attempt should be made to help him, or else he may not be able to function properly. Information on each child is necessary if a teacher is to teach and understand his children with any degree of success. A pleasant classroom climate will do much good. Teaching in itself is a big job. We cannot do everything the educators write in their textbooks. Admittedly, good guidance is a part of good teaching. A good teacher always gives a lot of personal guidance without thinking about it. Let's compromise. Let's take the parts of a guidance program that will help teachers and pupils the most and forget the rest. A compromise approach should include such special things as visiting each home and having each child write an autobiography (both done early in the school year); keeping anecdotal records on only the children with problems; using a sociogram a few times a year; and talking with children about the causes of their behavior. Teachers may want to add other specific guidance techniques.

Suggested Guidelines:

1. Teaching is a full-time job. Suggest some special guidance techniques and let the teachers choose the ones they want to use.

2. Good teachers have always used personal guidance. Boost the teachers' morale by pointing out the parts of a guidance program which they are already using. The list, which will surprise you, will include such things as cumulative records, standardized and informal testing, intra-class grouping, counseling, reports to parents, and sound promotion policies.

3. Start beating the drums for a full-time guidance counselor in your school.

DEFINITION OF CREATIVITY

"My teachers disagree on how they should treat a child's creative product. Some think a child's creative work, such as a story, should not be displayed if it contains mistakes in English mechanics or grammar. Other teachers think that a child's creation should be displayed without correcting the imperfections."

Put yourself in the child's place. You have completed a clay model of an elephant. The legs should have been shorter. The body could have had more girth. There are other minor defects. You tried to make it look like real. When you look at your created product, you think it does look like an elephant. You see those imperfections, but you say to yourself that you did your best. And you don't mind those mistakes. It's *your* elephant. You did the work. You know other children are more skillful in working with clay. You could have asked a friend to fix the head so it would look better, but then the elephant wouldn't be solely yours. It would be the product of the two of you. You accept the elephant the way it is. You're glad the teacher didn't try to improve it. You're proud of your work. And you feel good all over when the teacher makes a compliment about it, and puts it on the display table with all the other clay figures.

Suggested Guidelines:

1. A creative product is the work of the creator. Persuade teachers not to alter their pupils' creations or suggest improvements.

2. If a child's composition grows out of an English assignment, mistakes should be corrected and an evaluation should be made.

3. You will have to convince teachers that you like to see the actual creative product of children. Sell this concept to the staff. Two references for your help are *Creative Youth* by Hughes Mearns (Doubleday), and *Creativity in the Elementary School* by Miriam Wilt (Appleton-Century-Crofts).

ENRICHMENT AND REMEDIAL AREAS

"We have many enrichment and remedial programs operating in our school. My teachers complain that their basic instructional program suffers, since throughout each day certain children are leaving the classroom."

I sympathize with this problem; it is one of my pet peeves. In some schools the *extras* have so thoroughly saturated the school day that the *basic subjects* appear to be the extras. Daily at various times, different children leave the classroom to attend special classes for remedial reading, chorus, speech, and musical instruments. Although the basic need is for children to improve their use of the native tongue, 15—30 minutes a day is spent learning a foreign language, which will benefit less than one per cent of the children later in life.

That the school has a definite responsibility in some of these areas is unquestionable. But is it not true that any *one* of the basic subjects is more important than any *one* of the non-basic subjects? Any amount of time spent on the "frills" means less time to spend on the basic subjects. These "frills" have been merchandized to weak and gullible administrators by persistent and influential parents who measure quality in a quantitative way. Teachers should complain about their disrupted programs. Administrators should be careful what additions are made to the curriculum, for what is put in the curriculum today is going to be difficult to get rid of tomorrow.

Since parents pay the school bill, they have a right to suggest what they would like to have. But as their school executive, you have the obligation to advise and influence them in making decisions as to the soundness of their wishes.

If you can't prune some of the non-basic subjects, here are a few suggestions which may help you. Try to schedule the special offerings near the beginning or end of the school day. This gives a teacher a relatively large block of time in which all members of the class will be in the classroom. An extra could be held during part of the lunch period if there is enough time. However, be sure the involved children get five minutes to run their steam off before afternoon classes begin. Also before school officially begins—between 8:00 and 9:00 o'clook—and after school officially closes—from 3:00 to 5:00 o'clock—give three hours which are usually spent waiting for buses or on desultory activities. Second, limit the number of minutes a child can be out of the classroom. Work this out with the staff.

Suggested Guidelines:

1. Discourage attempts to add special enrichment and remediable areas which would be deleterious to the basic instructional program.

2. Don't add extras to the curriculum which the parents should provide for their children.

3. Use scheduling which minimizes classroom interruptions.

4. Limit the time a child can be out of the classroom for special activities and classes.

RETARDED CLASS EXCLUDED FROM SCHOOL LIFE

"Nobody knows my special class exists. We're left out of everything."

A basketball intramural league is organized for the boys of the intermediate grades, but the boys in the intermediate special class are not invited to be on a team. When the boys and girls of the special class go outside for recess, no one in the other classes invites them to play in the kickball game. Teachers of two classes on the same grade level often share films and filmstrips, but it is seldom that a teacher shares a film with the special class. A unit on Mexico will acquaint the pupils of the sixth grade with their southern neighbors. But in the culminating activity, which features a fiesta, no class member is aware that the boys and girls down the hall in the special class are virtually *unknown neighbors* who would be happy to join in the festivities. Also, the intermediate special class, because it has 9's, 10's, and 11's, is not tied to the fourth, fifth, or sixth grade in any way. They are out in the bleachers by themselves. Such slights are unfortunate, to say the least.

Why do these thoughtless things happen? Do teachers intentionally ostracize special classes? Is this planned? Or does it happen without anyone thinking about it? It appears that this educational sin is more an act of omission than of commission.

We agree that special class children need special consideration in academic instruction, but they also need special consideration in areas of human understanding. They are sensitive beings, just as we are. They have feelings and know when they are excluded. As a principal, will you try to have your teachers and pupils make these retarded youngsters a part of the school life? Will you help to give them a sense of belonging . . . of contributing . . . of sharing . . . of participating . . . of feeling important . . . ?

How can you do this? In faculty meetings, stress the importance of special classes in the school life. Ask the staff to make sure these children are integrated into the total school program. See that they are included in special auditorium programs, in viewing films, in recess games, in intramural sports, in contests, in clubs, in sharing culminating activities of the social studies, in field trips, and in science fairs. Be sure that they are given opportunities to participate in all school activities. Let them have a turn to do whatever all the other pupils do. Ask a teacher who is interested and whose classroom is near the special class to take the responsibility to see that the pupils are not bypassed.

Suggested Guidelines:

1. Point up to the staff the need for special class pupils to be a part of the school life.

2. Discuss with the staff the areas where improvements are needed to help the special class become integrated with the total school program.

3. Appoint a teacher to take personal responsibility for helping to integrate the special class into the total school program.

FIELD TRIPS

"My teachers do not make good use of field trips. They do not take many trips and they plan poorly the few trips they take."

There is an enormous amount of work involved in planning and taking each field trip. Contacts have to be ascertained and made, buses must be arranged for, permission gotten from parents, a road route determined, and the site previsited by the teacher, who must also familiar-ize himself with the content to be gleaned. These are a few of the numer-ous important planning activities. In addition, the personal liability of the teacher is increased from the time the bus leaves the school until it returns. Another fact to be taken into consideration is that an elementary school teacher is required to prepare and teach five or six different subjects a day. This background gives a clear idea of why teachers make so few trips in a school year.

To encourage and promote field trips, appoint a committee of teachers whose function will be to determine standards for trips, approve specific trips for specific grade levels, and develop a field trip guide. As you look below at the suggested guidelines, you may think it is a lot of work. It *is* a lot of work. Without the guide, each teacher would have to do the work himself. With the development of a good guide, the number of man-hours required in taking a trip is greatly reduced for each teacher. Once the work is done by the committee, the guide needs only to be kept up-to-date. You will notice that the guide contains almost all the information a teacher needs for taking a trip.

Suggested Guidelines:

1. Appoint a committee of teachers, preferably those who are well, acquainted with the immediate community and outlying areas, to:

a. Set up standards for field trips; *e.g.*, develop a standard-ized parent permission form, require that teachers pre-visit sites or locations, and establish a ratio of so many adults to so many children (a good ratio is one adult for every ten children).

b. Approve specific trips which correlate with instructions for specific grade levels.

c. Prepare a guidebook on field trips which includes the following information:

> (1) A list of possible field trips with name and telephone number of the person to contact for arrangements.
>
> (2) Road maps, hand-drawn or commercial, for each trip.
>
> (3) The location of eating and restroom facilities at and on the way to the site.
>
> (4) Times of special presentations and admission rates, brochures describing the site, and outlines of events or places to visit.
>
> (5) Content information in brief: significant facts, concepts, and generalizations which will enable the teacher to be knowledgeable about the site.
>
> (6) A list of things children should look for, and a few questions which they should try to find answers to on the trip.
>
> (7) Follow-up questions to be used by the teacher after the class returns to reinforce learning, correct misconceptions, and motivate further study.

RECESSES

"I have a few teachers who consistently take long recesses."

One of the advantages of the self-contained classroom which is pre-dominant in our schools is that it permits flexibility and elasticity in scheduling instruction. In departmentalized elementary school class-rooms, the instruction of subjects is fettered to the clock. Sometimes, during recess, a softball or kickball game will be reaching its apex when the recess time has run out. Is it not reasonable to take advantage of the factor of elasticity of the self-contained classroom to finish an inning, or to play a few extra innings if excitement and interest are at a high level?

There are some teachers, it must be admitted, who often take extra long recesses even though maximum recess times are stated in the handbook. One principal told me she overcame the problem by programming the outside bell to ring five minutes before the recess was over and five minutes after the recess was over. Any time between the ringing of the bells a teacher could terminate the recess at an appropriate place, but in any case the recess ended when the second bell rang. For one teacher who took recesses at irregular times, the principal of another school supplied a small timer clock, the kind housewives use for cooking. It is small enough to be placed in a pocket. Another principal told me she installed a large clock, protectively caged, on the outside of the school near the playground.

Also, if special teachers teach music, art, physical education, or foreign language at your school, you can schedule one of these classes immediately after recess is over. The teacher then feels a responsibility to be punctual for the special teacher.

Suggested Guidelines:

1. If recesses are occasionally long for good reason, acknowledge that this is one of the advantages of the self-contained classroom.

2. If recess times are abused, program the outside bell system, lend a timer clock, or install an outdoor clock.

3. Schedule special teachers, such as an art or music teacher, for the period after recess.

"I have a teacher who takes the recess in his room instead of permitting the children to go outdoors to run their steam off. Another teacher does not give her children any recess."

John Dewey in *Democracy and Education* states that, "a chief cause for the remarkable achievements of Greek education was that it was never

misled by false notions into an attempted separation of mind and body."
Recesses are imperative for elementary school children. Their bodies
require and demand recesses. Why do teachers not let their children go
outside? In most cases it is too much bother for the teacher. The teacher
may be lazy and does not want to line them up, take them out, supervise
them, bring them in, water and dewater them, and quiet them down.
An indirect hint to the teacher may be all that is necessary. "I'm glad to
see your children at the blackboard. Activities like this one, arts and
crafts correlated with social studies, and especially recesses outside help
the child to get some of these ants out of his pants. Keep up the good
work!"

For a few teachers who do not get the hint a more direct approach is
needed. Appoint a committee (the offender of course is on the committee) to study how teachers can meet the needs of the "whole child:"
social, emotional, intellectual, and physical. Or, delimit the study to how
teachers can meet the physical needs of children. Since this is a beneficial
topic for the entire staff, their findings and recommendations can be
presented and discussed in a faculty meeting.

You may want to draw up a recess supervisory schedule which will
have teachers rotating the recess duty. One teacher can supervise two or
three classes. Of course, in some schools this will be impossible; the type of
children will make it necessary to have each teacher supervise his own
class.

If the condition continues, then you as the principal will have to be firm
in dealing with the offender. Ask the teacher why he does not take a
recess out-of-doors when the weather is nice. Explain and discuss why
children need the benefits of out-door play, but be firm in your demands
that the children get a recess outside. The welfare of children has a prior
lien. If the teacher has a physical disability which prevents him from
going outside, he should exchange duties with another teacher.

Suggested Guidelines:

1. Use an indirect hint in which you explain the necessity of meeting
   children's physical needs.

2. Appoint a committee (of teachers) to study how teachers can
   meet the physical needs of children. Make the offender a member
   of the committee.

3. Draw up a recess supervisory schedule in which teachers rotate the duty.

4. If a teacher has a physical disability, have him exchange duties with another teacher.

5. If nothing else helps, talk to the teacher and be firm in your demands.

Sports

"I have teachers who only encourage their children to play three sports: basketball, softball, and football. A few teachers criticize children for making mistakes in games. We need an improved sports program."

There are some teachers who abuse children in the elementary school. The best advice I heard was stated by one of my favorite professors who truly understood the philosophy of the modern elementary school. He said that the elementary school is a practice school where children should not have to pay too dear a price for an error. It is the responsibility of a principal to promote this kind of thinking with his school staff.

Sports are important enough to children in the elementary school to warrant assigning a teacher who is sports-minded as the director of school sports. His function would be to introduce new recreational activities and games, to organize and supervise intra-mural leagues, and to purchase, distribute, repair, and inventory games and equipment. Varied sporting activities in the elementary school are needed to meet individual differences in muscular development and coordination. Jack may be a poor basketball player but an outstanding soccer player; Sharon may not be able to catch a softball but may be adept at ping pong; and Tyrone may be an inferior dribbler but a champion marble shooter. Baseball, football, and basketball have always been the big sports in schools—for those who could play them, and for others who could not but enjoyed watching them being played. But we also need soccer, volley ball, roller skating, kickball, badminton, ping pong, chess, tumbling, marbles, wrestling, shuffle board, crochet, checkers, pool, carroms, ring toss games, swimming, foot races, relay races, tug-of-war, whiffle ball, and other different activities.

Competition on one's age level helps boys and girls to develop in mind, attitudes, and body. But competition in the elementary school is limited to intramural leagues and unorganized informal play. Inter-school competition is out. Informal and non-formal competition is needed. The junior high is the proper place to begin school-versus-school sports. At this age the adolescent's development is ready for highly organized sports. Teachers tend to think intermediate grade girls do not have the coordination required for intramural league play. Although boys seem to have more agility and coordination for sports, from my experience, girls have both skill and interest, and need only a teacher to teach them a few rules, organize some teams, and supervise their play.

Suggested Guidelines:

1. Assign a sports-minded teacher as director of school sports.

2. Provide and encourage many different kinds of games, sports, and other athletic activities.

3. Encourage intramural competition among similar age groups. Organize leagues and tournaments, but prohibit interschool athletics.

4. Promote the philosophy among your teachers that the elementary school is a practice school where children should not have to pay too dear a price for an error.

SPECIAL AUDITORIUM PROGRAMS

"Should each class be required to give an auditorium program? Some teachers spend too much time trying to make the program a polished performance. Other teachers have little ability in this area. My teachers have asked me to scratch these programs. They want the Christmas and May Day programs eliminated, too, because the basic subjects suffer too much."

When I was a teacher there was only one aspect of the job that I despised: being responsible for one auditorium program during the school year. I would have gladly swapped that responsibility for painting the flag pole, or cleaning out the roof gutters of the school or anything else. Getting a program together was really a headache. My turn was usually near the end of the year. The thought of it haunted me from the first day of school until it was over. And when the time came to prepare and practice for the program, my instructional day was a complete loss. For two to three weeks the basic subjects were neglected or given little attention.

Let us discuss the class programs first. The children should have an opportunity to perform before an audience—to play an instrument, to play a role, to recite a poem—but these performances should be an activity growing out of what is going on in the classroom, or something of an enrichment nature. They should also be voluntary.

In addition to the voluntary programs of classes, in a large school the primary classes and the intermediate classes should meet separately for a special monthly or bimonthly auditorium program. All the classes could meet together in a small school. Leadership on a voluntary basis could be provided by pupils, teachers, parents or other resource people. Such programs could include "singspirations," a discussion of a current events topic, a travelogue, a demonstration of artifacts, a musicale in which children play instruments or classes sing favorite songs, teachers' musical talents, or the summer's travel slides of a pupil or teacher; the possibilities are unlimited. The meeting is informal, and what goes on takes little practice. The children are together as a school group; there is the feeling of school unity. Aren't these kinds of meetings more desirable than those that have to be practiced for weeks?

Now, let us think about the programs given on Christmas and May Day, programs that frequently involve one or two hundred pupils in a single play or musicale. You know why these programs are presented? That's right—for the parents. Now, are we in the business of entertaining parents? If not, then let us stay clear of such presentations. As a principal, do you know how many hours of work the Christmas play takes? The amount of pupil and teacher hours it takes represents the same number of hours that arithmetic, spelling, reading, and all the other subjects were neglected. Now tell me, is it worth it? And another thing—would you care to direct, control, and manage a hundred or more children for the next Christmas play? Take your choice: be the music director or the play director.

This is the Christmas program that took place at my son's school last year. As the Glee Club sang, the birth of Christ was silently re-enacted by pageant members. A few pupils played solos on their instruments, and the audience joined the chorus in a few Christmas songs. At another school an opaque projector was used to show the art work of children, Kindergarten through Grade Six, as the school chorus sang various songs. The preparation of these programs disrupted little instructional time. It seemed to me as if the staffs at these schools were wise in selecting such programs.

Suggested Guidelines:

1. ABOLISH: involuntary class programs; programs resembling Broadway production; programs requiring practice for more than one week; programs in which teachers have a *heavy hand;* programs involving large numbers of children.

2. ENCOURAGE: voluntary, informal, short class programs which are a result of on-going classroom learning, like short plays and skits; monthly or bi-monthly programs for the whole school or part of the school, which include "singspirations," discussions, special kodochrome slides, and resource speakers.

PARTIES AND MORE PARTIES

"One of my teachers has a party almost every month."

Parties benefit children in many ways. There are many social benefits: children learn how to serve refreshments, how and when to use the proper manners, and what to do when something spills. They learn responsibility in planning, executing, and cleaning-up. They share with their peers the goodies they have brought from home, and there is the recognition of special days and accepted customs of the larger society in which boys and girls live. Of course, class parties are fun; tension is released and physical freedom is enjoyed.

But having a party is a privilege not to be abused. A party is not to be used as an excuse to avoid the regular chore of a work day.

Suggested Guidelines:

1. State in the handbook the three or four allowable parties for the holidays that the staff chooses. Suggestions: Halloween, Christmas, Valentine's Day, Teacher's birthday.

2. Limit parties to an hour.

3. Recognize the benefits of a class party: the social benefits; the recognition of special days and accepted customs in the larger society in which children live; the enjoyment and the release of tension.

INTERRUPTIONS OF TEACHERS

"My teachers think the P.A. system is used too often."

If they think the public address system is being used too often, no matter who is using it—you or the school secretary—you had better control its use. This problem can be serious. Imagine yourself as the teacher with the P.A. system constantly interrupting your carefully planned lessons. Perhaps the interruption is for less than a minute; nevertheless, the lesson or activity suffers. If it happens two or three times a day or more, it becomes irritating. Many general announcements not of immediate import can be written on the teachers' check-in and check-out sheet, thus eliminating the disrupting noise.

Let the teachers teach! Unless there is an emergency, don't interrupt them. Usually anything you have to say to the teachers can wait until after school. **Let them teach** . . . If there is a telephone call for a teacher, tell your secretary to inquire if it is an emergency. If it is not, the secretary should tell the caller the teacher is in the classroom with his children. The secretary should offer to take a message, or state that she will have the teacher return the call during his free time.

Messengers can be another problem. Most of these messages can also wait until after school. Sometimes school letters or notices to parents are delivered to classrooms—more interruptions! You can place these letters where teachers check in and out of school and the teachers can take the number they need. If materials have to be delivered to classrooms, have deliveries made during the first and last fifteen minutes of the school day. This rule of thumb applies to all interruptions.

Suggested Guidelines:

1. Restrict interruptions—telephone, messenger, and P.A. system. Use the P.A. system only when absolutely necessary. Have deliveries made during the first and last fifteen minutes of the official school day.

2. Use the bulletin board where teachers check in and out of school for announcements.

3. Honor the instructional day. Don't shut down or interrupt production except for emergencies.

TEACHER-PARENT CONFERENCES

"A few of my teachers want a parent-teacher conference with each parent once a year. Some of the other teachers say that conferences with parents don't accomplish much."

A parent-teacher conference is one of the best reporting techniques in use. You must be aware of its value. At such a conference, there can be a mutual exchange of certain important information about a child which would never be put into writing—both positive and negative remarks. Questions are asked, explanations are made, and misunderstandings are cleared up.

If the staff appears to be divided on this issue, you will want strong support from some quarter before you do anything. Discuss the topic at a school board meeting. Or, if you're in a large school district, consult your supervisor. Make a strong case for it. Have a proposed plan ready. You will undoubtedly get support, and then you are ready to make a move.

There are several plans which I have seen schools use. One school uses classroom conferences an hour before each P.T.A. meeting. Then, about the middle of the school year, one evening is set aside for conference appointments. The school sends the parents a form letter. Later, it is returned indicating whether or not the parent will keep the appointment. The conferences begin at four o'clock, and each parent is allotted ten minutes. The room mother remains outside the classroom. She has a list of the appointments and admits parents to the classroom. She also reminds the teacher when ten minutes have elapsed, if another parent is waiting. The school board provides a free dinner for each teacher.

At another school the teachers make two appointments for each morning—8:30 to 9:00—and two appointments for each afternoon after school is over. This is done in the middle of November and in the middle of March. Still another school dismisses children at noontime and schedules appointments for conferences in the afternoon.

Suggested Guidelines:

1. A teacher-parent conference is the best method of reporting child progress.

2. Teacher-parent conferences should be by appointment; also, they should be private.

3. Select the plan which has the strongest teacher support:

    a. Conferences from 4:00 P.M. to 9:00 P.M.
    b. Conferences a half hour before and after school.
    c. Conferences from 12:30 P.M. to 5:00 P.M.

P.T.A. ATTENDANCE

"A few of my teachers go home after the P.T.A. meeting instead of having refreshments and mingling with the parents. Some don't attend the P.T.A. meeting, but leave after the classroom visitation preceding the meeting."

Personnel problems such as this often occur because there are no policies to cover the situations. Each year a principal needs to be alert to areas requiring written regulations or clarifications of policies. The contents of an effective teachers' handbook should be revised periodically. As situations arise, additions, revisions, and clarifications should be made to keep the handbook current.

State your policy in the handbook. Teachers should remain for the P.T.A. meeting and the refreshment period afterwards. This is one of the few times when a teacher can talk with many of the parents. It is one of the best times for a teacher to develop good public relations. No matter how skillful the teacher is, during the school year there always arise problems which without the background of strong parent-teacher rapport could easily become compounded through misunderstanding, impetuosity, and self-interest. Strong parent-teacher rapport is beneficial to many school-wide programs, such as proposed changes in the curriculum or voting for school bond issues. Teachers need a wholesome relationship with parents, for he never knows when he will need their support. If a parent were to bring the serious charge of negligence against him, the accused teacher would be most grateful to have support from his other students' parents. **A good parent-teacher relationship is a must!**

The P.T.A. is a parent-teacher organization. If the teachers fail to support it, the organization becomes a parent organization. Most P.T.A.'s are parent dominated. Teachers need to play more of a role in the group. Perhaps the absence of a *role* is why many teachers do not actively support the group. If the P.T.A. is to be a bona fide organization of parents and teachers, the teachers should be members of P.T.A. committees and be represented in the slate of officers. Otherwise, why should the teachers become interested in the group?

Suggested Guidelines:

1. State in the handbook that teachers are expected to attend all regular and special P.T.A. meetings and to stay for refreshment times which follow. Teachers who wish to be excused should notify the principal so their absence may be accounted for.

2. Discuss with the staff the advantages of teachers developing good public relations with the parents of their students.

3. Use your influence on the executive committee of the P.T.A. to give teachers more identity in the P.T.A. through committee membership, assignments, and officership.

Parent Interruptions

"During the school day, I have noticed on a few occasions a teacher talking to a parent about her child in the hall outside the classroom."

The instructional day is sacrosanct. It should not be interrupted, even by the P.A. system, if possible, and certainly not by a parent-teacher conference. State in the handbook that teachers are to refer to the office all parents who come to their classroom during the instructional day. The teachers will be grateful to you for this policy. What teacher wants to be interrupted while he's teaching? What is the value of a parent-teacher conference about *one* student when thirty children need supervision?

Post a notice on every school entrance door that parents may confer with teachers before and after school. Be specific. State the times: for example, from 8:30 to 9:00 and after 3:30. At the beginning of school send a letter home which contains this policy. Require that parents stop at the office before seeing the teacher. The office is the nerve center of the school. It is the key to all the classroom doors. Encourage parents to make an appointment ahead of time so that the teacher will be prepared for the conference.

Suggested Guidelines:

1. Honor the instructional day. Keep interruptions to a minimum.

2. In the beginning of the school year, notify parents of visiting policies.

3. Post on the outside doors of the school the times when teachers are available for conferences.

4. Encourage parents to make conference appointments with teachers, but only at the specified hours.

Teacher Deficient In English

"Last month one of my teachers sent home to the parents a letter describing a future class activity. The next day two parents called me and one parent

came to see me about the grammatical mistakes and misspellings contained in the letter."

A teacher may do a good job, but have his reputation changed overnight by sending parents a letter that contains mistakes in the use of the language. When it happens, the reputation of the entire school suffers. Many questions are raised in the minds of parents about a teacher who is teaching their child the English language, but hasn't mastered the rudiments himself.

Establish the policy—and put it in writing in the teachers' handbook— that *all* mass correspondence must be cleared through the principal's office and countersigned by him. Don't give the letters a cursory inspection; scrutinize them carefully. Your signature will indict you also if there are mistakes. If you are not sure or there is a question in your mind, use a teacher in the school who is skillful at English to check each communication to parents. You should still countersign each letter. The benefits from this procedure go far beyond the mere mechanics of expression. In the first place, it tells parents you support the substance of the letter. And second, it forces teachers to show you each letter that is sent to parents. You will be aware of what's going on, and, also, you will have control over what will go on.

Suggested Guidelines:

1. Establish the policy that all written mass communication has to be countersigned by the principal.

2. If you have to, enlist the aid of a teacher competent in the use of written expression.

TEACHERS WHO DO TOO MUCH FOR CHILDREN

"I have a couple of teachers whose rooms are very attractive. The bulletin boards are outstanding. The room displays are eye-catching. Wherever cutout lettering is used, it is perfect. The only fault is that the teacher has had a heavy hand in nearly everything."

One important reason a teacher wants an attractive classroom is to please the principal. Sometimes teachers become so involved in the activities of their classrooms that they often do more than they intended to do. It's up to the principal to persuade teachers that students should do the work. Usually all teachers use a heavy hand at some time or another, but some use a heavy hand all the time. Talk briefly about it at a faculty meeting; tell the staff you would rather see pictures hung crooked by children than hung straight by the teacher. Remind them they had their chance at first or fifth grade, or whatever grade they are teaching, when they were children. Now as a teacher, it's their job to motivate and guide. In short, to step aside and let children have their rightful chance to develop bulletin boards, build constructed models, make displays, cut out letters, hang pictures, mix colors, solve their own problems, make their own mistakes, and, if possible, to correct them.

After such a talk, teachers will know they don't have to have a *perfect* appearing classroom. Later, when you visit classrooms, compliment something done which looks as if the children had little help from the teacher. Tell the teacher how glad you are that she let the children do it.

Many teachers have special talents and seek means of displaying them for self-satisfaction and recognition. You may fulfill this need by giving them a specific job in the school so that their talents may be used. For example, the teacher who has artistic ability may be asked to arrange displays for the bulletin board in the teachers' lounge. Other teachers can take care of the display cases near the entrance of the building. Whatever the talent, make sure it is being used in some way, but not at the expense of the child.

Suggested Guidelines:

1. Tell the teachers in a forceful way that you like to see decorated classrooms which are the result of *children's* work, and not teachers' efforts.

2. Compliment teachers on specific evidences of the practice of this philosophy in practice.

3. Think of jobs around the school which can use the talents of teachers.

CHILD TRANSFERS

"When a new child is taken and introduced to the assigned teacher, invariably certain teachers will exclaim, 'What, another one?' What can be done to discourage these negative remarks?"

Transitions are disrupting. When we move to a different area, the carefully planted and cultivated roots of our existence are torn asunder. The place we move to may be similar or totally different from our last abode. At any rate, there are many adjustments which have to be made. Children as well as adults have to make these adjustments. The main concern of transplanted children is their new school, particularly **that first day**. Many questions crowd their minds: What kind of school is it? Will my teacher be nice? I wonder if the kids will like me? Does the principal give lickings? I wonder if the work will be too hard? I wonder what they do at recess time? These and a hundred more questions trouble children. For the child, **the first day is most important**. When a teacher greets a new child with, "I guess I have to take you," it is high time to take some action which will make transitions easier, especially as far as the child is concerned.

Discuss with the staff how important it is to make a new child comfortable in his new school milieu. Develop with the staff some routine guidelines which are to be followed when a new pupil arrives at the school. Some suggestions are:

1. If possible, notify the teacher who gets the child at least a day ahead of the child's arrival.

2. Have the secretary introduce the child to the principal and the classroom teacher.

3. Ask the classroom teacher to assign a buddy to the new child. The buddy takes the new child on a tour of the school plant during which the non-professional staff and school specialists are introduced.

4. In the classroom, locate the new child near his buddy and in a comfortable social setting; a girl would be seated next to girls and a boy next to boys.

5. The principal visits the new child in the classroom on the first day; he makes another visit about one week later.

6. The principal sends a greeting to the parents of the child explaining the school's program. Accompanying the letter are any important school messages which the principal sent to other parents prior to the new child's entry.

If these or similar guidelines are followed, a new child's entry into a school will be a pleasant experience. The early communication between the principal and the parents will answer some of their questions and certainly allay some of their fears.

Transfers *out* of a school are important also. In this case, a check-off form could be necessary if specialists are used. Before obtaining a transfer card from the office, a child would have to certify that all his books and materials were turned in. This would entail getting the signatures of the librarian, cafeteria worker, art, music, and homeroom teachers.

Suggested Guidelines:

1. Discuss with the staff the importance of smooth transitions for child transfers.

2. Develop steps which will ensure smooth transitions:

   a. Notify the teacher in advance of the child's arrival; assign a buddy to the new child; tour the school plant; arrange a comfortable seating location; follow-up the transfer personally; communicate with parents of the child.
   b. Include a routine to be followed for transferring out of a school, if it is needed.

Children Who Come Early To School

"My teachers want the school doors locked in the morning until a half hour before school officially begins. They say that some children come to school too early and run wild in the classrooms."

Whether the school doors could be locked until a half hour before school starts depends on the type of school situation that exists. In a neighborhood school where all pupils walk to school, it could be done. A junior or senior high school could do this because the students are old enough to remain out-of-doors by themselves. But young children are clearly not mature enough to stay outside without supervision, and cold or wet weather presents other serious problems.

Usually children come to school early for two good reasons. A father is on his way to work and drops the child off at school because no other transportation is available, or he does so to avoid the child's waiting for a bus in inclement weather. Second, children are early birds because they have positive feelings about the school and want to get there as soon as possible each morning. The first of these reasons is sound; the second is highly complimentary. Is it not better to have the children enjoy school and come early, than to dislike school and be late or absent?

Some arrangements have to be made for early arrivers, though. A standard policy could be that children who arrive in the morning before the teacher is in the classroom are to be seated at their desks. The teacher could post an assignment on the board for these children. If the number of children who come early warrants it, they could all report to the room nearest to where the busses unload, and the teacher on bus duty could supervise them. The teacher on bus duty may have to come a little earlier to school to do this.

Suggested Guidelines:

1. Recognize that there are sound reasons for children coming to school early.

2. Accept the fact that children are probably safer in the school building than outside where moving vehicles are a danger.

3. Make standard rules for early arrivers.

4. Schedule the teacher on morning bus duty to come early and supervise the early arrivers in a room near where the busses unload.

Injured Or Ill Child

"A fifth grade boy suffered a leg abrasion in a softball game. The nurse cleaned and bandaged the wound. The parents learned of the wound a few days later when infection set in. The parents complained that the nurse or teacher should have notified them on the day of the accident."

When children are under the care of the school, there is an obligation on our part to report to the parents any information which appears to require follow-up at home. And certainly injuries—even though they may be minor ones—should be reported. The nurse at one school telephones the parent of every child who comes to the health room for treatment. Also, a form letter describing the injury or illness is sent home with the child. The parents, after signing the bottom of the letter stating that they have read it, return the letter to the nurse. The nurse also has a log-book which contains anecdotes on children treated. The parents of this school appreciate the interest the school has in their children. It goes without saying that the parents have confidence in the staff at this school.

Suggested Guidelines:

1. Recognize that it is the school's obligation to report any injuries and illnesses to parents.

2. Provide a procedure which notifies parents of hurt or ill children.

    a. Notify the parents by telephone.
    b. Write letters describing the accident and the treatment. Request parents to sign and return the letters to the school.

3. Require the nurse to keep a log-book which lists the name of each child treated, the date, time, treatment given, and follow-up data relevant to the parent, the child, and the school authorities.

RELEASING CHILDREN

"A sixth grade girl brought a note signed by one of her parents requesting that she be dismissed at 2:00 o'clock for a dentist appointment. A teen-age boy arrived at the school in a car and the girl left with him. A few days later it was learned the parents had not written the note, that the girl did not have a dentist appointment, but did have a boy-friend who drove a car."

This could have been serious. A procedure for dealing with releasing children should be firmly established in every school. When a student brings a note requesting his early release from school, the writing should be checked against the parents' writing on file—the application form, excuse notes for absences, and signatures on report cards. If a parent telephones the school and requests a child's release, immediately a return call should be made to the home to verify if the person making the request was really the parent. Parents will appreciate this precaution and concern for their children.

No release of a child should be made without the principal's approval. If the person arriving to get the child appears to be a stranger, the child should be asked in private if the person is known to him. If the child has older brothers or sisters in the school, have them verify the identification. When the home has no telephone to verify questionable written requests, I ask the stranger for identification and write his name, license number, and car description on my calendar pad, although the child has identified the person as his older brother or uncle. If after this there is still a serious question in my mind, the child is not released.

Suggested Guidelines:

1. Approval of all releases of children is given by the principal.

2. Verify handwriting of notes from previous specimens found on records: writing on application forms, excuse notes for absences, report card signatures.

3. Verify telephone calls from parents requesting release by immediately telephoning the home.

4. Ask the child privately to verify a questionable guardian who arrives for the child.

5. Require the questionable guardian to produce identification cards; note the license number, make and color of car, when telephone checks are impossible or fruitless and the child knows the caller.

6. Don't release the child, if you seriously question the stranger. Notify the police.

Clerical Work

"My teachers complain about the amount of clerical work they have to do. They say they were trained and hired to teach, not to perform these and other low-level functions."

A recent study stated that nineteen per cent of a teacher's time is spent on miscellaneous work, *i.e.*, preparing report cards, attendance registers, and other records. Twenty-nine per cent of a teacher's time entails out-of-class instructional activities. Only for fifty-two per cent of the time was a teacher engaged in actual class instruction! How deplorable! If a time and motion man discovered this to be true of a job in industry, do you think any changes would be made?

Modern school systems guarantee to teachers that little of their time will be spent performing the duties of a clerk. The well-to-do districts use electronic computers, and the poorer districts employ clerks for record-keeping functions. I suppose the long and the short of the problem is what value we as principals place on a teacher's instructional time. Many times we could let the school secretary do these routine jobs. We decide whether a teacher will collect money for lunch, charity, candy sales and banking. Also, the teacher has to tally and score teacher-made and standardized tests, prepare attendance register reports and hectograph and mimeograph copies, and often dust shelving and wash blackboards. Do other professional people perform these kinds of work? Do doctors and lawyers personally type and send bills to their clients? Do they personally collect money from their clients? Do doctors assist the orderlies in cleaning up the operating room after the surgical procedure is over? Do the prosecuting and defense attorneys take turns sweeping out the jury box and dusting the court room? Doctors and lawyers spend their time doing the things which their education has trained them to do, not the minutiae of their work. Education in some areas, I am ashamed to admit, is a Johnny-come-lately. If we are to regard our field as a profession, then it seems to me our standards, policies, and behavior should be consonant with such a high calling.

Suggested Guidelines:

1. Value a teacher's time as you would that of a professional person.

2. Shunt the clerical work of teaching to non-professional employees.

3. Entertain ideas of electronic computers for preparing records and reports. Cooperate with other school districts in developing such a program and pro-rate the costs.

LATE REPORTS

"I have a few teachers who are always late in handing in reports."

No matter how simple or difficult a report may be some people always get their reports in last and late. Set a deadline for each report; this enables teachers to budget and plan their time. I realize, however, that deadlines perhaps will not solve the problem entirely. Some teachers always turn in their reports two or three days after a deadline. Don't get upset over this—it won't do much good. You cannot change these people, for they just don't live by deadlines; they are always late for appointments, too. And besides, this is such a small matter. Be patient.

What you can try is setting a deadline a few days before the actual deadline. For instance, if the school monthly attendance report has to be in the country office on the fifth calendar day of the new month, tell the teachers the deadline for handing in their monthly report to you is on the first day of each month. A reminder on the teacher check-in sheet will help some teachers to remember.

Suggested Guidelines:

1. Set early deadlines so *your* deadlines will be met.

2. Recognize that some people are poorly oriented to time.

3. Be patient; being late is not really too serious.

RESEARCH QUESTIONNAIRES

"Occasionally a request is made by a university or a doctoral student for permission to conduct a research project in our school. My teachers are reluctant to cooperate with these studies."

The teacher is asked to fill out a questionnaire which says there will be no identification of teachers. If a teacher doesn't fill it out, in a few weeks he receives a postcard reminding him to kindly do so. Unless the returned questionnaires were coded in some way, how did the researcher know the teacher had not returned his form? Some procedures are necessary to carry out research, but integrity should be placed high on the list.

Research is an important tool. It is an instrument that helps teachers do their jobs better. Its purpose is to dig a little, to uncover evidence, to describe current practices, to make comparisons of outcomes under different conditions, and to make recommendations for change. Research is never used to get evidence about a specific teacher or to make teachers insecure; nor is it used to embarrass teachers or to frighten them. Tell your teachers this, because it seems that teachers do not want to take the time to fill out a questionnaire because they don't fully appreciate the benefits of research.

These teachers may lack confidence in what they're doing. How long has it been since you praised your teachers? Do they know you have confidence in them? Have you ever reassured them that their methods are sound? That they are doing a good job? Do you rarely use praise because you think teachers will get "swelled heads?" If this is so, you don't understand the value of praise very well.

Build your teachers up. Be specific. Tell them precisely what they have done that is commendable. When teachers know their superior has confidence in them, they are not afraid of research. It is only when teachers are unsure where they stand with the boss that research raises some disturbing questions.

Suggested Guidelines:

1. Reassure your teachers that they are doing a good job. Praise teachers for specific things. They will try to do even better. They will have confidence in their work and they will trust you.

2. Explain to the staff the close relationship and benefits of research to teaching. Encourage them to cooperate with research. Promote research in your school.

CHARITABLE COLLECTIONS

"A few teachers have asked me why charitable collections have to be made in schools. They think it is the role of the home to teach children to share their resources for helping others."

It seems that values are not taught in schools. Values of sharing, character, morals, discipline, and religion are relegated to a minor role in relation to the emphasis placed on intellectual values. How significant a contribution can an intellectual but dishonest man make? The McGuffey Reader of yesteryear is remembered for its marked concern for teaching integrity and building character. Since the Reader was generally discarded there has been an obvious neglect of instruction in ethics and values by our public schools. When a charitable collection is taken in the schools, the value of helping others to fight disease and poverty is instilled. The teaching of values is the indisputable role of the home and the school. Let us recognize this.

But we also recognize that charitable collections can be overdone. No more than two or three collections should be made in a school year. Be careful which collections you support. A teacher may request that his favorite charity be included. If you support his favorite charity, you may be pressured by other teachers to include their favorite charities. Decide with the staff which two charities will be selected. In a large school system this is usually done by the administrative council. The selected charities should be meaningful and of interest to all the pupils. You may wish to change the charities each year in order that children may get acquainted with the various needs and services of mankind.

Whichever charities are selected, try to be sure that the collection procedure does not make extra work for the classroom teacher. Ideally, if an announcement for the collection is made on one day, the collection can be made the following day.

Suggested Guidelines:

1. Recognize that collections for charities can teach the values of cooperatively and collectively sharing one's resources with a specific area of mankind's need.

2. Limit charitable collections to two or three a year.

3. Select with the staff the charities to be supported. The staff may desire two different charities each year so the children become aware of a variety of ways of helping people.

4. Ensure that children understand the objectives of the chosen charities.

5. Make the collection a brief operation. Announce the collection one day; collect the following day.

6. Eliminate any teacher work attached to the collections.

FIRE DRILLS

"My teachers do not regard fire drills seriously. What can I do?"

Well-executed fire drills require planning; children and teachers must know what is expected of them. Draw a diagrammatic sketch of the school showing fire routes from each room in the school. Include this in the teachers' handbook under the section Fire Drills. Post a 3 × 5 index card giving the fire drill routes on the door of each classroom and special room. Include the following information in the teachers' handbook: how teachers and children should conduct themselves; windows closed; lights extinguished; coats left behind; routes to be taken; locations outside; accounting for children with the attendance register; and re-entering the building. After each fire drill, announce over the public address system the general positive and negative aspects of the drill. Any individual criticism should be given to teachers privately.

I know a principal who was faced with this problem of teacher indifference to fire drills. He solved the problem by having the teachers conduct the fire drills. Each month a different teacher has the responsibility for the drill. She pulls the alarm, inspects the empty building, checks and accounts for all children, and completes the written report. The teachers look on the drill a little differently now. They know that this is serious business. They feel responsible for conducting well-executed drills. Now, "Miss Jones" knows that all teachers are required to conduct a fire drill. She also knows that *she* will have to conduct a drill, sooner or later. Realizing this, she is more cooperative with other teachers who have been assigned drill duty. This plan helps teachers to become aware of what to do in case they have to give the alarm for an actual fire. It also quickens their senses to the importance of this life-saving activity.

Suggested Guidelines:

1. Plan the routes and policies of fire drills. Each teacher's handbook should contain this information.

2. Post on each classroom door and on the doors of special rooms a 3 × 5 card on which is printed the route to be followed in case of a fire.

3. Give a critique of each fire drill over the public address system immediately after classes return to their rooms; praise publicly; criticize individual teachers and classes privately.

4. Assign teachers the responsibility to conduct fire drills.

GRADUATION

"One of my two sixth grade teachers is pressuring me for a formal graduation for the children in June. I subscribe to one public school graduation: the one that comes at the completion of high school."

So do I. Some nursery schools have formal graduations, and believe it or not, I've seen pictures of kindergarteners wearing mortar boards. If elementary, junior high, and senior high schools have graduations, a student could have as many as five graduations in thirteen or fourteen years. If a child can graduate from nursery school to kindergarten, and from kindergarten to first grade, why can't children graduate from first grade to second grade . . . and so on through each grade level? In short, if it is graduations we want, this plan would give us one for each year spent in school. Is this what we want? The absurdity of the idea is obvious.

There are several good reasons for graduation at the conclusion of twelfth grade: public education usually includes twelve years of education; in most states children are required to attend school until they are sixteen; and many students will terminate their formal learning after the twelfth grade. For these reasons, it seems logical that the first graduation should be held at the senior high school level.

Suggested Guidelines:

1. Use your influential powers to dissuade teachers and parents from wanting graduations in the elementary school.

2. Be firm. Stand for what you believe. Don't let parents or teachers inveigle you into this utter nonsense.

4

Problems Involving

Discipline and Duties

In some schools the difficulties discussed in this chapter are minimal. The teachers have few problems of discipline mainly because their instructional planning is thorough, appropriate to interest, and challenges the children they are teaching. The bus, cafeteria, and playground duties are carried out with competence and dependability. The lunch program operates smoothly. The management of supplies and equipment presents no serious problems.

However, in other schools these areas are sources of concern to the principal. They may appear banal and less important than other problems treated thus far, but any problem is serious to the person it affects. The seemingly small problem of a single teacher can have grave repercussions among other teachers in the school, and can seriously disrupt part of the school program.

What can a principal do if teachers rely on him to discipline their children? How can a principal assure himself that the use of corporal punishment will not be abused by teachers? What can be done about teachers who are lax in performing their duties? Should a teacher have to make up a money shortage in a lunch report? How can the principal manage wisely the thousands of dollars of equipment and materials under his supervision? As with the other problems discussed, these require skill in human relations and sound judgments about what is good for the total school program.

CHILD SENT TO OFFICE

"There are two teachers on my staff who frequently send children to my office. I suspect these teachers think that when disciplining is needed, the principal should do it."

A policy for handling disciplinary cases is needed. The larger the school the greater the need for this policy. The roles of the principal and teachers should be clearly defined. A principal does not have time to talk with children who have committed petty offenses; this is the job of the teacher. Unless the offense is serious, a teacher should make an attempt to deal with the offender himself.

Many principals have a disciplinary report form which has to be filled out by the teacher before a pupil referral is made. Because filling out the report takes more than a few minutes to complete, minor offenses are seldom reported. Here are some items included on one report form:

1. Describe, completely and specifically, pupil's offense, using anecdotes for each separate offense.

2. Describe the teacher's attempts to deal with each separate offense. Be specific.

3. Describe the home and the home environment.

4. Describe the attitude of the parents, and state any pertinent suggestions or information they have given you.

5. Summarize all standardized test data contained in the cumulative records. Include the following data: name of test, year of test, child's chronological age at time of test, and test results.

6. State the number of days absent for the previous and current school year.

7. Give two dates when you are available for a conference with the principal.

These items indicate that some action has to be taken by the first line of authority—the teacher—before a child is referred to the principal. If the offense is serious enough to be considered by the principal, the background information on the above report is necessary. Teachers do not go to the trouble of filling out a report unless the misbehavior warrants it. Notice that the parents have to be contacted by the teacher; this conforms to the chain of command discussed in another section of the book. Also, the home has to be visited. If the teacher and the parents are unable to solve the problem, then the principal comes into the picture.

Some teachers need more help than others with discipline problems. In a large school, to alleviate the burden on the principal or assistant principal, a teacher on each grade level could be appointed as the consultant for disciplinary problems. The disciplinary report could be initially sent to this consultant. Extra compensation should be given if the case load becomes heavy during the school year. Only cases which are unresolvable at the consultant's level are referred to the principal.

Be flexible about the guidelines—sometimes a pupil's unruly behavior warrants sending him directly to the office. If this be the case, have the teacher send him to the principal's office immediately. This is preferable to having the child remain outside the classroom in the hall, where he is under no one's supervision.

Suggested Guidelines:

1. Let minor infractions be handled by the teacher.

2. Require teachers to keep anecdotal records for recurrent misbehavior cases.

3. Encourage teachers and parents to make the initial attempts to solve problems.

4. Ask teachers to submit the disciplinary report along with requests for help from the principal.

CHILDREN WHO ARE KEPT IN

"Should teachers be permitted to deprive children of their recess?"

The fact that you raise the question makes it obvious that you have some reservations about this practice. This is a good sign. A recess is given for a specific reason: to benefit the child. His body needs it—he has energy to burn. Seldom can adults sit and study more than an hour at a time. We are told that frequent rest periods—5 to 10 minutes every hour —are better than long periods of study followed by long periods of rest. What is good for adults in this case is even better for children. A child's body builds up a "head of steam" faster than that of an adult. When a child is denied a recess for whatever reason you can be sure that "pressurized steam" is going to find a way out, and it will probably happen after recess in the classroom. He will get out of his seat to go to the pencil sharpener or water fountain, supposedly. On his way, he will fool around, take his time, "goof off," or maybe jokingly hit someone. If he stays at his seat, his productivity will be of no significance because the needs of his physical body have been neglected. In short, he will be tense, restless, inattentive, and intractable. Keeping a child in at recess affects many persons: the particular child, the other pupils, and the teacher. This traditional disciplinary method, which is fast becoming obsolete, is not practiced by good teachers. Discourage it in your school. Get James Hymes' book, *Behavior and Misbehavior*, for the professional library at your school, if they do not already have a copy. This is one of the best writings available on child misbehavior. As you read it you will become acquainted with an up-to-date philosophy. Circulate the book among your teachers. Discuss the book with your staff.

If a teacher is adamant in depriving children of recess, request that she take the child to the playground where he may stand and observe other children enjoying the recess. This prevents the child from being left in the classroom unsupervised. When recess is almost over, the child should be permitted to jog three or four hundred yards so that he can use up some of his energy before returning to the classroom.

Suggested Guidelines:

1. A recess was put in the school day for a purpose. Have your teachers honor it just as they honor the teaching of arithmetic or reading.

2. Never permit a teacher to leave a child unsupervised in a classroom.

3. Purchase *Behavior and Misbehavior* by James L. Hymes, Jr., Prentice Hall, Inc., Englewood Cliffs, N.J. Discuss the book with your staff.

CHRONIC CHILD MISBEHAVIOR

"How can I help a teacher with a child who continuously misbehaves?"

When a child continuously misbehaves, some serious questions are raised. Does his misbehavior have its roots in the home? In the school? Within himself? Or in all three—home, school, and child? The cause or causes have to be found. If the trouble is in the home, talk to his parents and see what improvements can be made. If you think his maladjustment is psychological, seek help from your pupil personnel worker, school psychologist, or a child psychiatrist from a local social agency. Use the team approach if the problem is a severe one.

Quite often the trouble is in the classroom. Some possible explanations are: the boy needs recognition; the work is above or below his ability level; or he is an isolate or a rejectee. Also, poor planning by the teacher may be the reason. Observe the child in the classroom . . . keep anecdotes . . . avoid making any snap judgments. Does he have a history of misconduct? What did his former teachers think about him? Check his cumulative records.

I know of a case where the teacher and the parents of a problem child worked together. Occasionally the teacher was invited to dinner by the family, and twice the teacher accompanied the family to church. The teacher took the unruly boy to dinner and went bowling with him one night. The boy responded to the teacher's interest in him; he sensed that his teacher and parents were taking definite steps to help him. He was embarrassed that his misbehavior was the cause of their concern. The teacher showed him love and care—the boy needed this—and his behavior improved. TLC (tender loving care) has potency; used wisely and discreetly, it has a positive effect on persons of all ages. We tend to like the people who like us and make us feel important, and the relationship of a boy to his teacher is no exception.

Do not expect a boy with a history of misbehavior to change in a week or a month. The basic causes of his behavior must be found. The right kind of treatment can bring about change, though it may be gradual. Too often, a wholesome rapport between the teacher and a child is the only agent needed to bring about a marked change in behavior.

Suggested Guidelines:

1. Find the causes for the misbehavior. Observe the child's behavior in the classroom. Examine cumulative records and talk to his former teachers.

2. Use the case study approach. Collect and weigh all available data on the child and his parents. Find out his peers' attitudes toward him. Check the organization and difficulty of the classroom work in relation to the child's abilities.

3. Give the teacher a copy of *Behavior and Misbehavior* by James L. Hymes, Jr., Prentice-Hall, Inc., Englewood Cliffs, N.J.

4. Encourage the teacher to take a definite interest in the child and to work with the parents.

5. Recognize that change is slow; the teacher needs to be patient.

6. Determine the relationship between the child and his teacher; perhaps a transfer may be needed.

CORPORAL PUNISHMENT

"In our state the teachers can administer corporal punishment. Some parents strongly complain about a few teachers being too harsh. Can you suggest some guidelines which will ensure its wise use?"

If your school has no guidelines for the use of corporal punishment, **get some soon!** Problems of serious consequences can arise between the teacher and the principal, and between the parents and the school, when physical punishment is permitted; therefore, stated policies are a must.

I do not normally subscribe to corporal punishment by teachers. The law protects murderers, thieves, and rapists from being physically assaulted or harmed by law enforcement officers. Yet too often, some parents inflict unreasonable physical punishment on their children from cradle age **until** adolescence—the time when the child's strength is beginning to equal that of the parent, and some teachers see corporal punishment as the panacea for all behavior ills.

There are some children who will benefit from a spanking; the number is small, however. Some educators suggest that corporal punishment be used as a last resort. Why should corporal punishment be condoned only after other techniques have failed to correct misbehavior? If a method is approved to correct misbehavior as a last resort, then its use, it seems, should be approved as a first resort. A procedure does not warrant endorsement merely because another procedure has failed. The use of a measure has to be based on its own merits. Is it effective? Does it change behavior? Can it be used legitimately with children? Corporal punishment has prevailed since biblical times. The familiar "take him to the woodshed" idea is found in Proverbs 22:15: "Foolishness is bound in the heart of a child; but the rod of correction shall drive it far from him." Ideally, some children would benefit from a firm slap on the buttocks as a first resort.

However, if corporal punishment is permitted in your school, some specific guidelines for its use should be established to protect you and the teachers. Since this topic is a volatile one, these suggestions pertain to every use of corporal punishment. This check list will discourage indiscriminate use of this measure to correct unruly behavior.

Suggested Guidelines:

1. The teacher is strongly convinced that corporal punishment is needed and will benefit the child.

2. The punishment occurs soon after the misbehavior.

3. Administration of punishment is witnessed by another teacher.

4. The teacher administering the punishment is unemotional and in a sound frame of mind. He does not administer the punishment in a malicious and vindictive manner.

5. The punishment is administered privately.

6. The reasons for the punishment are stated and understood by the child before the punishment is given.

7. The punishment fits the crime. It is reasonable and fair. The age, maturity, and sex of the pupil are considered.

8. The buttocks receive the damage.

9. After the punishment, the child is encouraged to behave better by the teacher for specific reasons which are understood by the child. The child is accepted back into the classroom by the teacher and pupils since he has paid his debt to society.

10. The principal and parents are notified on the same day that the punishment occurs.

TEACHER-PUPIL PERSONALITY CLASH

"In November a teacher requested that a girl in her room be transferred to another fifth grade in the school because their personalities clashed. The teacher admitted that the child's minor misbehavior often seemed worse than it actually was. The teacher found it difficult to be objective in her dealings with the child when such a pronounced bias was present."

Some colors are uncomplementary. Various foods do not go together. Even furniture of different periods clashes. And so do certain personalities. The teacher in the above example recognizes and accepts the fact that she and the child are incompatible. Both suffer, and, as a result, the class suffers also.

The initial action of the principal is to try and convince the teacher that the best action is for her to try and make an adjustment to the situation. She will be a stronger teacher if she can do this. If the teacher is unable to make the adjustment, transfer the child to another fifth grade class. The principal should make an appointment with the parents before the transfer is made and tell them that, for the welfare of the child, a transfer is necessary. The parents will want to know the reasons. State them openly. Don't hedge—be positive. Speak in a complimentary way about both teacher and pupil. Avoid taking sides with the teacher or the child or being critical of either one. Follow up the discussion with a letter to the parents.

Suggested Guidelines:

1. Attempt to have the teacher adjust to rather than evade the situation.

2. Recognize that some personalities are incompatible.

3. Make an appointment with the child's parents to discuss the proposed transfer. Speak positively about the child and the teacher at the conference. At separate times during the conference have his *old* and his *new* teacher meet the parents.

4. Transfer the child to another classroom without explanation to the pupils of the involved classrooms.

5. Confirm the transfer in writing to the parents.

Bus Duty

"*My teachers don't take bus duty very seriously. Some teachers openly neglect it. Others don't stay near when the busses load or unload.*"

Bus duty is perhaps the most important duty a teacher has. If proper precautions are not taken, a child's life can be wiped out in a few seconds under a bus wheel. A teacher-friend told me he saw a school bus start to drift backwards when it was unloading one morning. The rear wheel hub came within inches of a small boy who had just gotten off. This school did not have teachers on bus duty in the morning. The teacher related the near miss to the principal. And what was done? Nothing. To my understanding, this particular school still has no teacher on bus duty in the morning. If it is considered essential to have a teacher on bus duty in the afternoon when busses are loading, is it not equally important that a teacher be scheduled for duty in the morning when the busses are unloading? Without question, teachers should supervise the loading and unloading of busses at all times.

Devote a faculty meeting to the topic of improving bus safety. Don't point up the laxity of teachers, but rather stress the importance of bus duty. Cite some accounts of recent bus accidents. Talk about the things that can happen when busses are loading and unloading children at your school. Discuss the potential dangers in and around the areas used by the school busses. Examine the bus safety program from many different viewpoints: for example, children coming in from recess near the area where the busses are arriving; blind corners of the school building where the busses come around; playground areas on which busses travel; the responsibilities of the teacher on bus duty; parents' cars in bus areas; the relation of children who walk to school to the busses; problems of the safety patrol; and the problems that arise when the teacher on bus duty is absent or late. Explore these topics and others relevant to bus duty and child safety.

Prepare an evaluative form listing the various areas of bus safety, and pass this on to teachers. Have them rate the school program and offer suggestions for change Appoint a committee to study bus safety problems, and name an interested teacher to chair the committee. Hold a faculty meeting to discuss the committee's proposals for promoting bus safety. Do not treat this vital topic lightly—develop with the staff definite policies to save life and limb.

Suggested Guidelines:

1. Devote two or three faculty meetings to an examination of your school bus safety program. Hand out printed sheets which suggest areas of concern. Have teachers rate the school's bus safety program. Cite some bus accidents. Solicit oral and written suggestions for improvements.

2. Appoint a committee to study the problems of bus safety. Discuss their proposals and recommendations at a faculty meeting.

3. Whatever plan is used, establish with the help of the staff definite procedures and regulations to be followed. A copy should go into the teacher's handbook.

4. Contact a principal who has a good school bus safety program in operation. Invite him to speak to your staff about safe-guarding the lives of children.

Cafeteria Duty

"My teachers do not want to be responsible for cafeteria duty. They say they need a lunch time away from the children."

Some state laws guarantee women a thirty minute rest after 4 or 5 hours of work. During the school day teachers need a few rest periods. Elsewhere in the book I have advocated occasional 5–10 minute breaks during the school day at which time a teacher may smoke, duplicate materials, or just plain rest. At this time, supervision of children is done at long distance or by the neighboring teacher. In the upper grades, a responsible child can be assigned to monitor the room.

I approve of teachers getting away from children during the lunch hour. A rest in the middle of the day regenerates the teacher for the afternoon. Some schools use parents to supervise the cafeteria and the playground during the lunch hour. Where parents are carefully selected and the children are properly instructed as to the authority of the parents' role, the plan works satisfactorily.

Parents are an excellent source of help. They are eager to assist the school, and their service is *gratis*, too; but, in the main, their talents and service go largely untapped. It appears that teachers as a whole resist parents assisting or participating in any part of the instructional day. If this is an accurate observation, the reasons for the resentment need to be uncovered, and attempts should be made to correct this unhealthy attitude. Experience has shown that parents can make a significant contribution to the ongoing of the school program. The school must be alert to this and should provide opportunities for their help or services.

If the teachers are adamant in their disapproval of parents supervising the cafeteria, then there appears to be no alternative except to assign the teachers themselves and all other professional personnel to this task. The cafeteria has to be supervised by some one. A principal could supervise it, but this arrangement never works out too well. I know a principal who does it but wishes he had never started the practice. He seldom gets a rest either before or after the lunch hour, and he is fettered when parents or visitors stop by at lunch time to confer with him.

If teachers must supervise the cafeteria, they have to accept the duty as part of their job. No job has all of the odious parts picked out of it. If possible, schedule *all* the professional people in the building: the art, music, foreign language, physical education and special education teachers, the librarian, nurse, and assistant principal. If everybody helps, no one will have to serve too often.

Suggested Guidelines:

1. Teachers should have time to eat their lunch, free from the responsibilities of supervising children.

2. Parents are a good and dependable source of assistance for school programs. If the teachers approve of their help, appoint a dependable parent to organize and administer a Parent Patrol program: to solicit and sign up parents, to construct schedules, to get substitute parents, and to clarify the duties of the parents.

3. If for some reason parents cannot help, distribute the assignments to as many professional people in the building as possible. This decreases the number of times a teacher has to serve.

PLAYGROUND DUTY

"How can I impress upon my teachers the importance of playground duty? The teachers are late getting on the playground; they stand around and talk with other teachers, and they don't stay in the vicinity where the children are."

The most vivid way to quicken teachers' senses to the importance of playground duty is to cite a legal case in which a playground accident resulted in a teacher being taken to court on the charge of negligence in performing this duty. Any comprehensive book on school administration will outline some specific principles which courts generally uphold in cases of this kind.

You should speak to the staff about the topic of legal liability. Legal liability is a grave thing. Your uninsured car can be totally demolished in an accident and you can lose almost $4000. Your uninsured home can burn to the ground and your loss is limited to its value. But legal liability is another thing—only the sky is the limit! If an uninsured teacher is indicted and convicted on a charge of negligence of duty, depending on the awarded damages, the court can attach his check the rest of his life. Put these facts before the teachers. Be unequivocal and forceful. A teacher who is not negligent in performing playground duty watches over the children as if they were his own. A wise principal has guidelines for playground duty listed in the teachers' handbook. Some guidelines are suggested:

1. Teachers are to be in the immediate vicinity of the children.

2. Teachers on playground duty who stand and talk together during the recess are considered to be not really supervising recess activities, even though they are present on the school grounds.

3. Teachers are considered by law to be the parents (*in loco parentis*) of the children under their supervision, and should act in the reasonable ways in which parents normally act: children's coats and jackets are on and buttoned in cold weather, children are kept out of water or wet fields, and hazards of play and of the playground are looked for and eliminated.

Since the school is directly responsible for the safety of children entrusted to its care, you may want to investigate the school's playground safety program the same way as was suggested above for the bus safety program.

Suggested Guidelines:

1. Discuss legal liability and negligence of duty with the staff. Cite some actual cases involving negligence of teachers for support.

2. Establish guidelines which closely follow principles the courts usually uphold in negligence cases.

3. Investigate the school's playground routines and practices for possible improvement.

INABILITY TO PERFORM DUTIES

"Sometimes a teacher is unable to perform his duties. He may have a conflict after school with bus duty and a committee meeting, or a parent may unexpectedly stop by just before he goes on playground duty. Is it the principal's responsibility to find a replacement when such instances occur?"

A safe answer is no. The principal may be out of the building at the time when a replacement is needed. Furthermore, whom would a principal ask? Would it be fair for him to impose up on another teacher? Who wants to fulfill somebody else's duty? A sound policy is to require the teacher who cannot perform his duties to find his own replacement. He can later reciprocate by serving in another's stead.

Suggested Guidelines:

1. Require the teacher who has the scheduled duty to provide his own replacement if he is unable to meet his obligation.

2. Remind him that "one good turn deserves another."

UNWILLINGNESS TO PERFORM DUTIES

"One of my teachers flatly announced to me that she was not going to perform her cafeteria duty."

Upon hearing such a remark, the principal is likely to get upset and go on the offensive. Avoid this, at all cost. Tell yourself that in dramatic cases like this almost always somebody has said or done something which hurt the feelings of the teacher. Arrange a conference with her. Humor the teacher. Be pleasant, relaxed, sincere, and understanding. At the outset, tell the teacher you appreciate the excellent cooperation she has given in the past . . . that her teaching has made a fine contribution to the school. Compliment her for a few of her special accomplishments. Then subtlely find out the reasons for her decision. Accept her ideas by restating them. Sympathize. Empathize. Often when the reasons are known, some remediable action is possible. And, if the situation is dealt with effectively and prudently, the teacher will be back on cafeteria duty the next time her turn comes up. If the circumstances of the situation preclude her taking the cafeteria duty, you may have to find a teacher who is willing to exchange bus duty for cafeteria duty with the involved teacher. Use your skill in human relations to resolve this problem.

Suggested Guidelines:

1. Control your temper. Stay away from the panic button. This is only one of many personnel problems which you will face as a principal.

2. Arrange a conference with the teacher; compliment the teacher on her accomplishments; find out the reasons for her decision. Empathize with her. Take appropriate action to resolve the problem. If the teacher still refuses, a mutual exchange of duties with another teacher may be necessary.

3. Recognize that even good human relations may become strained occasionally.

LUNCH COLLECTIONS

"The teachers complain about collecting money for lunches. They say that someone in a non-teaching position should do it. Can you suggest some alternate plan?"

I agree with the teachers. This should be done by a non-teaching staff member. The teacher has enough to do in the morning getting ready for instruction. The only responsibility a teacher should have in this area is to send to the office the lunch count for each day. Too many clerical functions are placed on teachers. Here are two simple plans which have worked satisfactorily in elementary schools. In the first plan, the children pay a cafeteria worker when the class goes to the dining room to eat. A child who forgets his money may charge the meal. But he must pay for his meal before he can charge another. Otherwise, the school would be involved in a sizable loan and collection business. Of course, if a child needs a lunch and owes for a lunch, you will instruct the cafeteria worker to give him a bowl of soup. No child should go hungry.

In the second plan, lunch tickets are purchased. One or more central booths sell tickets daily, 20—30 minutes before school starts. A child can buy several tickets. Parents would be glad to be responsible for the sale of tickets. Primary children feel grown-up when tickets are used. The use of tickets helps to teach responsibility too. Print your own tickets, or have the high school printing shop make them for you.

Suggested Guidelines:

1. Attempt to have non-professional people perform clerical duties so that teachers can do what they are hired to do—teach!

2. Use the plan which the teachers favor. Suggested plans are:

    a. Children pay at the counter as they go through the lunch service area.
    b. Tickets are sold; one of the parents controls the sale of tickets.

LATE LUNCH REPORTS

"In the morning a few teachers are always late getting the lunch report to the office."

Suggested Guidelines:

1. Program the school bell to ring fifteen minutes after school officially opens. Remind your teachers that lunch reports are due on or before the bell's signal.

2. Be patient; A late lunch report is the cost of having teachers collect lunch money.

Money Shortages

"What is the proper action to take if money shortages appear in the lunch report?"

Suggested Guideline:

1. Notify the teacher of the amount of shortage discovered. If she cannot rectify it, make an adjustment in the report listing the unpaid lunch(es) as free. This is another clerical cost of having teachers to collect lunch money.

Free Lunches

"Who should determine which children receive free lunches?"

Suggested Guidelines:

1. The teacher or the school nurse should investigate the home conditions and determine the children who need this help. Then a report is usually given to the principal or assistant principal who makes the final decision.

2. Children who receive free lunches should be required to perform some kind of task, regardless of how insignificant it may be. Usually he is glad to wipe off lunch tables for repayment of his dinner. A child will thus become work conscious instead of welfare conscious if this practice is followed. Also, the child will have positive feelings about earning his own way.

Teacher's Lunches

"Teachers complain about their lunches. They don't like paying more than the children do and receiving the same food and the same portions. How should I answer this complaint?"

Much of the school food comes from the United States government in subsidized surplus food programs. This food is for school children primarily. Thus, because of this subsidy the cost of children's lunches is low. There are always nominal costs attached to operating cafeterias. Frequently, cafeterias operate in the red. Teachers on salary should bear some of the costs. It is highly unlikely that teachers could buy a similar lunch platter as inexpensively at a restaurant. Teachers as well as children should be able to obtain extra helpings, because often there are sizable quantities of food left over and thrown away.

Suggested Guidelines:

1. Explain to the teachers that the school lunch program is a government subsidized food program for children. Teachers should pay more than children.

2. If possible, provide larger portions; add an extra dish, a salad, coffee, and second helpings for teachers. No person can put forth his best efforts if he is hungry.

Over-Used Supply Items

"Some teachers complain that other teachers over-use certain supply items; therefore before the end of the year, the items are exhausted."

In both large and small schools this kind of complaint is common. If a current inventory is kept on file, when an item gets near the low level it can be reordered. The low level of an item is based on the length of time it takes to receive the stock, the supply hours, and the rate of consumption of the item. Invariably, primary teachers use paste heavily; and intermediate teachers use a disproportionate amount of construction paper. I grant that some teachers waste certain supplies and that others abuse the privilege by not using materials judiciously or economically. But frugality for frugality's sake is not a virtue. Whenever supplies are used wisely for learning experiences, no matter in what quantity, there should be no restriction. This is what the supplies are for—to be used to help children to learn. When items are used intelligently, there can be no "over-use."

The amount of consumption of an item in one year should indicate how much should be ordered for the next year. If you do not keep a current inventory, retain copies of the teachers' requisitions, and use these as a guide for ordering. There are some supply rooms stocked with items which have not been requisitioned in five years. If care is taken when the yearly supply order is developed, widely used items will be ordered in larger quantity, and little used items will be eliminated from the list.

Suggested Guidelines:

1. Keep a current inventory on stock items; establish a low level so that replenishing is done at regular intervals to avoid depletion.

2. Estimate the consumption of items in one year; use the estimation to determine the projected usage for ordering supplies in the future.

3. If the stocked items are used to support an effective instructional program, do not be concerned about *over-usage* by any teacher; there is no such thing.

4. Know the "users" from the "abusers."

INVENTORIES

"Our school lost a new filmstrip projector last year, and each year many books are unaccounted for at the end of the year. How can I gain better control over these losses?"

The value of school equipment and books would astonish us. More amazing would be the laxity which many elementary schools exercise in their inventory and care of school materials. In some elementary school neighborhoods, the high school boys regularly walk through the school grounds after school is over, looking for basketballs, soccer balls, bats, and other athletic gear left on the playground. Equipment disappears and nobody realizes the loss until months later. Thousands of dollars are spent on books. They are distributed to teachers, but nobody is held accountable for their loss. The absence of inventories is a weakness in many elementary schools.

In well-managed schools, the principal has a master inventory sheet. His teachers sign for books and learning aids in September. The children's books are numbered and the children are held responsible to the teacher for them. Equipment is kept under key at night. When items are missed the principal is notified. Inventories are taken at the end of each school year. In some schools, inventories are conducted at the middle and end of the school year. While the teacher cannot be held wholly responsible for missing items, since there are always many persons coming in and going out of classrooms, he can be held negligent for not taking reasonable measures to protect, control, and account for the materials under his supervision.

An inventory is essential for a number of reasons. It establishes an accurate insurable value for the contents of a school. If a school fire occurs, the inventory would be the substantiating proof of loss. Inventories also assist the principal in determining the needs of a school for the following year. Control and responsible management over the materials of instruction should be enforced.

Suggested Guidelines:

1. Conduct an annual inventory in June. Have teachers adjust their last year's inventory report for items added, deleted, or discarded; in this way, an inventory can be maintained with a minimum amount of work.

2. The principal who is responsible for the inventory of all materials of instruction delegates responsibility to the teachers for materials under their supervision. In September, the teachers sign for their materials. The teachers, in turn, delegate responsibility to the children for the materials which are distributed.

3. As principal, you are directly responsible for the careful management of all school properties—including buildings, equipment, books, and supplies—which the taxpayers have entrusted to

your keeping. You will perform your duty well if you treat and manage these possessions as if they were owned by you personally.

Wasted Electricity

"My teachers leave lights on in their rooms when they go to recess or lunch."

This is a common problem which would solve itself if teachers were billed for the electricity used in their classrooms. When someone else pays the bill, there isn't much incentive to remember to throw the light switch off. Verbal persuasion probably won't help much. You will get better results if a 3 × 5 card, on which is printed in large letters "PLEASE— LIGHTS OUT WHEN THE CLASS GOES OUT," is posted at eye-level on the inside of each classroom door.

Suggested Guideline:

1. Post a printed reminder on the inside of each classroom door.

5

Teacher-Teacher

Relationships

A principal can enjoy excellent rapport with members of his staff, only to discover one day to his chagrin that a lack of teacher-teacher cooperation and unity is undermining and deteriorating his efforts to conduct an efficient school-wide program. He learns there are many internal personnel problems between members of the staff. For example, two teachers had a heated argument a year ago at one school, and have not spoken to each other since. There is a young married couple at the school, and the wife strongly suspects that a couple of young, attractive teachers are attempting to inveigle her husband into acts of adultery. Another teacher forbids any other teacher to discipline her children. In this aura of contention, what can the principal do to help establish good interpersonal relations? If similar situations exist in your school, do not despair; remedial action is possible.

The responsible person to take the action is you, the principal. It is common knowledge that many principals do not want to get involved in disagreements between teachers. They think it unwise to jeopardize their satisfactory relationships with teachers by attempting to settle disputes or petty differences between members of the staff, but the principal has the unquestioned obligation to run his ship and to run it well. This means taking actions and setting policies which will enable teachers to work together with each other cooperatively and get along harmoniously.

Often teacher-teacher misunderstandings are caused by the absence of administrative direction. A good principal knows the high positive correlation between teacher-teacher unison, and the effectiveness of the school program demands that he become involved, whether he wants to or not. He must work to bring about good interpersonal relations. Ever aware of this necessity, he will take appropriate steps to ensure intra-staff cohesion and solidarity.

CLIQUES

"It doesn't matter what the rest of the teachers want; our clique is larger."

Wherever numbers of people are gathered, certain persons are drawn into the company of certain other persons. Because of some specific harmonizing factors people are attracted to each other. Gregariousness is a well established trait of men and animals. There will always be a few loners, but for the most part, people like people. Interactions of small and large groups are appealing and desirable. Fraternizing with a group gives people a certain kind of satisfaction and identification—two basic human needs impossible to obtain individually. It is thus that, sociologically, the group benefits its members.

Teacher cliques are obvious in small and large schools. The membership characteristics vary widely. One often finds smokers or non-smokers, traditionalists or progressives, and local residents or outlanders getting together. Even if a principal wanted to—and it is doubtful that he would —he would find it difficult, if not impossible, to disintegrate one of these exclusive social sets. In strong cliques each member protects his own interest in the group by defending the honor of other members of the group. Otherwise the group would eventually dissolve itself.

The question, of course, is how does a principal handle these cliques. First, he recognizes that they exist, that they have influence, and that they must be reckoned with. He learns who the leaders are. He discovers their sentiments, attitudes, and inclinations. He has a fairly accurate idea of how each clique will react to almost any of his proposals. And so, because the mainstream of thinking for each group varies somewhat, the principal carefully shapes and hones his proposals so that they will be acceptable to all cliques. He avoids pitting one group against another; this would be clearly seen by voting, so he does not use voting. He strives for consensus, works for unanimity, and encourages compromises. He seeks support and respect for minorities.

To spawn fresh and creative ideas the principal must be sure that the membership of school committees cuts across clique lines. He knows that certain school-wide projects will promote cooperation among all members of the staff. His committee assignments are governed by this fact. When the members of a group do something which needs correcting, the principal should speak to each member individually. Although he is aware of the various operating cliques in his school, the principal must never give a particular group any status by recognizing it in an overt way; this would have the undesirable results of honoring a faction and contributing to the deterioration of school solidarity.

Suggested Guidelines:

1. Be alert to the cliques in your school.

2. Discover the chief characteristics of membership in each group; be cognizant of the mainstream of their thinking; know their leaders.

3. Shape and hone your programs and proposals to cope with the varied thinking of these groups.

4. Sponsor school-wide activities and projects which will require and foster cooperation between cliques.

5. Give no public recognition to cliques.

6. Strive for consensus; respect minorities.

TEACHER-TEACHER ANTIPATHY

"That teacher graies on me. I wish she would get pregnant. Maybe her husband will get transferred by his company soon."

In an earlier chapter we discussed the clashing personalities of the teacher and pupil. It happens between adults too. Often time erases the sting of most disagreements. Sometimes the antipathy is unknown to the other person. In other instances, one teacher will say something derogatory about another teacher; later it is found out. Women in these instances are unpredictable. There could be an acrimonious confrontation in which aspersions are cast from each side. If this happened, it is not unlikely that open hostility or smoldering embers would be a lasting problem.

Such strong dislikes overtly affect the people and the program in a small school. There are some alternatives for dissolving the feud. The principal can talk with each teacher privately and explain how the school environment is affected. He will seek the causes of the antipathy and attempt to have each teacher understand and tolerate the other. If both of the teachers show some indication that they are willing to forget bygones, call them together and congratulate them on their wise decision.

A principal can have a conference with the two teachers. Often when the reasons are brought out in the open, misunderstandings are cleared up and issues are found to be groundless; at this point a skillful principal can reunite the teachers. In the event that an amicable settlement of differences is impossible and the antipathy is affecting the school program seriously, transfer both of them to different schools in the district. Don't threaten to transfer them if they are unwilling to forget the past. If you threaten them, they may agree to forget their differences, but will they get along satisfactorily? This is the question. If they would not bury the ax before the threat, then probably the cut is a deep one.

How to handle this problem in a large school depends on how often the two teachers must come into contact with each other; this will be too often if both are on the same grade level. Their strained relations would disrupt efficient grade level planning. For instance, their recesses and lunch hours are usually held at the same time, and their classrooms are in the same area; thus, contact between the two is almost unavoidable. A transfer in this instance would be necessary if they cannot be on friendly terms. Two teachers harboring ill-will toward each other with class-rooms on different sides of the school may be tolerable.

Suggested Guidelines:

1. Realize that good rapport between people can be disrupted by seemingly innocent words or acts.

2. Appraise the seriousness of the feud and the effect it has on the two teachers, other teachers, children, and the total school program.

3. Attempt to reconcile the involved teachers if hostility is overt. Talk to each privately; if both are willing to bury the ax, get them together and congratulate them for their sound judgment.

4. Separate the teachers; assign each to classrooms on opposite sides of the school.

5. Transfer both of the teachers to different schools if the situation warrants it.

TEACHER DISCIPLINES ANOTHER TEACHER'S CHILD

"Don't discipline my children. You take care of yours and I'll take care of mine."

An attitude like this on the part of teachers can lead to serious con-sequences. Sometimes a teacher will say to his class, "Don't pay any attention to Mrs. Charleyhorse. If somebody is going to discipline you, I'll be the one." If this is the prevailing attitude toward discipline, the children can run in the halls, skip steps, fight, commit almost any kind of offense with impunity. Unless their own classroom teacher observes and apprehends them, they will feel free to do as they choose.

Children require constant supervision. The more the better. Reasonable teachers recognize that to have control of children at all times requires

the cooperation of all teachers. Draft a statement for the teachers' handbook similar to this statement taken from a school's handbook.

> All teachers have the responsibility for supervising
> children regardless of which grade a child is in. While the
> homeroom teacher has a prior lien in the supervision of
> his children, the over-lapping of authority of plural teach-
> ers on the school's enrollment ensures maximum control
> of the student body.

Suggested Guidelines:

1. Tell your teachers that if the school is to have control of the
   children, then each teacher has the responsibility to help supervise
   all the children.

2. State that each teacher has priority over the discipline of his
   assigned children, when they are under his supervision. An art
   or music teacher has the responsibility to discipline children who
   misbehave while under her direction, or when seemingly unsupervised in another area of the school.

3. Encourage teachers to honor the disciplining of their children by
   other teachers.

4. Include a statement on this topic in the teachers' handbook.
   Make it clear that *all* teachers have responsibility for supervising
   all children.

Teacher's Class Disturbs Adjacent Class

"With all that noise next door, I wonder if they ever do any schoolwork!"

Unfortunately, some old school buildings and some recently constructed ones have classrooms which are not sound-proof. Through the
walls of some classrooms travel the sound waves caused by students and
teachers writing on blackboards, teachers' shoutings, pupils' hammering,

sawing, jumping, running, and yelling. To eliminate some of these things would be to stifle the hard-won advances which have been made in elementary education in recent years. Not that noise in a classroom is a good indicator of quality-learning experiences; nor that the absence of noise in the classroom is a predictor of acceptable methods and high achievement. But the learning activities of modern education emphasize the learning by doing approach in which a child's whole self—physical, social, emotional, intellectual—is considered. And when children do things today in school, they usually make more noise than the children did yesteryear when they sat and listened or wrote. The teachers know this, but stating it occasionally will help some traditional teachers to understand that the noise next door is not merely noise for noise sake! It is noise produced in connection with learning and growth. This should encourage traditional teachers to de-emphasize passive activities. Indicate in the teachers' handbook some suggestions for treating this topic.

Nevertheless, sometimes the noise does become too disturbing. A thoughtless teacher will abuse the privilege. Frequently doors are left open when noisy activities are going on inside. Closing the door would help; and, scheduling the noisy activities when the adjacent class has a recess would also aid in solving the problem.

If the weather is favorable, many of the activities such as dramatic play, sawing, and hammering can be done out-of-doors where the noise cannot reverberate and is easily absorbed into the open space. Other activities can be held in special rooms—the cafeteria, auditorium, speech and music rooms, library, or an unused basement space. Encourage teachers to use such spaces.

Suggested Guidelines:

1. Do not strive to eliminate noise produced in connection with an acceptable learning activity. The advances in education are often cases of weary hard-won battles.

2. State the relationship of noise to learning. It may cause a few teachers to shake some of the dust of traditionalism from their feet.

3. Request that teachers close their classroom doors when a noisy activity will disturb other classrooms.

4. Encourage the use of the out-of-doors for classroom activities, when feasible.

5. Make the following rooms and spaces in the school available for active and noisy activities: cafeteria, auditorium, speech and music rooms, central library, and spaces in the basement.

CONFLICTS IN USE OF SPECIAL ROOMS

"I don't know when my class can rehearse the play. The auditorium is always being used."

The use of special rooms does not have to be a problem. Have the school secretary construct a large calendar from chart board for each month and post it in a central location. Teachers can make reservations for the music room, the auditorium, or other special rooms by merely writing in the name of the appropriate room, and the date and time the room is desired. The principal should establish standard priorities however. For instance, a class which is scheduled for an auditorium presentation should take precedence over other classes in using the auditorium for the week preceding the program. Also, if films are shown in the auditorium only, the weekly audio-visual schedule for the various grade level divisions should be automatically honored. If necessary, the cafeteria or other empty rooms and spaces can be used if the demand on special rooms becomes too great.

Suggested Guidelines:

1. Post a large chart board calendar in a central location. Have teachers write in reservations for special rooms.

2. Establish standard priorities to ensure continuity of school-wide programs.

3. Make available any empty or unused rooms and spaces, such as the cafeteria, central library, or basement spaces, if the desired space is in use.

Teacher Critical Of A Specialist

"I know music, and the music teacher doesn't teach my children anything."

In this case, to borrow a phrase, a little learning is a dangerous thing. Many classroom teachers who are familiar with no more than the mere rudiments of music assume they know what a music program should or should not include. These "Know-it-alls" present a problem. Another personnel problem to cope with arises when the classroom teacher accompanies his class to music and remains with the class throughout each music period. This problem is discussed in Chapter 3 under "Special Enrichment Teachers."

The main problem here is not one of music but one of ethics. Does a teacher have the professional prerogative to criticize a colleague in the presence of other teachers? A code of ethics for teachers which I saw recently strongly decried the practice. The principal is the proper authority to determine whether a teacher is performing satisfactorily. If any teacher appears to act in a way which is seriously suspect, teachers are obligated to report their observations to the principal. This is not tattling! This is having respect and concern for the teaching profession. Ideally, the principal should supervise instruction adequately to determine where weaknesses exist. Although he may supervise adequately, he is usually oblivious to a malpractice, unless a parent or a teacher discloses it to him. An investigation of some complaints, however, will reveal the criticism to be groundless.

Suggested Guidelines:

1. Discuss the entire area of professional ethics with the staff. Use the state code of ethics for teachers as a guide. Obtain the national code of ethics from National Education Association, 1201 Sixteenth St., N.W., Washington 36, D.C.

2. Supervise instruction adequately. When people know they are being supervised, they tend to do their best work. When people know that the boss does not closely supervise them, they have a tendency not to put forth their best efforts.

Cupid At Work

"Have you noticed what's going on between Miss Smith and Mr. Brown? They even take their classes out to the playground for recess at the same time each day!"

Nothing better could happen to keep alive the hopes of unmarried teachers than a love affair between two faculty members. Each unmarried female teacher who entertains romantic ideas hopes that the next male teacher to be employed will be her knight in shining armor. Observing couples in love is a vicarious experience for some teachers. As principal, be careful what you do. An unintentional act on your part which appears to others to thwart or discourage Cupid will cause you to be labeled an ogre. Don't talk about the romance to anybody and avoid joking about it with either of the two involved teachers, because the romance may turn out to be a short-lived one. If it culminates in marriage, the staff will want to give the couple their blessings in the form of a wedding shower.

Suggested Guidelines:

1. Be circumspect in your attitude and actions toward the couple. Do not do anything to discourage or encourage the romance.

2. Don't discuss the love affair with anyone. It may be an ephemeral affair or it may culminate in marriage.

3. Have the faculty and staff give the couple a shower to express their blessings.

Husband And Wife In The Same School

"I had a slight dispute with Mr. Jones yesterday about his class disturbing my class when they go to recess. This morning when I greeted his wife in the faculty room, she ignored me."

There are a few good reasons why a husband and wife should teach at the same school, one of which is that the problem of transportation to and from school is eliminated. However, there are a number of reasons which militate against the success of such an arrangement. In the first place, it is not good for the couple. Too often, unfair comparisons are made by the teachers; for instance, the wife may happen to excel in sports and the husband may happen to lack coordination. Or the wife may speak with ease before a group and the husband may fear addressing an audience. Sometimes the husband may be proficient in an area in which the wife is weak. Such human shortcomings often contribute to unjustifiable estimations of a person's effectiveness. But over and above these there are factors of greater import that demand consideration. A quarrel in the home can be continued on the job. Teachers could find that they were forced to take sides, and an unhealthy climate could develop. An altercation between the wife or husband and another teacher or the principal would compound problems of human relations. Another instance may be the meaningless and harmless levity and camaraderie of female teachers with the husband or male teachers with the wife. Such innocent behavior can often arouse the groundless suspicions of the mate and foster ill feelings toward the suspected teachers. Many school boards faced with this problem have established policies requiring that a husband and wife be assigned to different schools, unless special circumstances demand otherwise.

Suggested Guideline:

1. Because husband and wife relationships with each other and with other teaching personnel sometimes compound certain difficulties and occasionally invite other problems of on-the-job human relations, it seems wise not to assign the husband and wife to the same school.

6

Teacher Abuses

and Negligences

In all vocations there are employees who abuse certain privileges and neglect assigned and specified responsibilities. Teaching is no exception. This section deals with one group of topics which are incontrovertible cases of abuse or negligence and which must be dealt with by the school administrator. You will notice that most of the solutions proceed from indirective to directive methods.

Intermingled are topics which the writer does not really think are teacher abuses, but which have been included because there are some principals who label them as such. Some principals think that teachers over-use a faculty room, rarely permit teachers to leave school early or to enjoy a cigarette except at recess or lunch-hour, and expect teachers to be on time in the morning and never to leave their classes unsupervised. It is this group of so-called "abuses" which causes a principal to alienate himself from his staff.

A principal would do well early in his career to prepare carefully a working definition of the word "professional." The thesis of the writer is that since teaching is one of the professions, its membership should be accorded the benefits of such a distinction.

TALE CARRYING

"I have a teacher who often has a rumor or tale to be dropped. She exaggerates stories and causes unrest and friction among other teachers."

This teacher needs attention and recognition. More than likely her attempts to receive recognition from her teaching have been fruitless. She tells tales and spreads rumors. She finds that this works whenever she feels a need for attention; therefore, she exaggerates an incident, stretches a truth, or simply fabricates a story. This teacher can stir up a beehive of activity in the school.

Often a teacher will carry a tale to the principal. The tale-carrier becomes an informer in an effort to make his position more secure. Such a person is often in search of other tales, which he can spread, hoping to gain more recognition. Always remember that "The dog that carries a bone will also drop a bone" is still true. So beware of all bone carriers!

One action is to try to meet the needs of this teacher through acceptable means. There must be some one thing which the teacher does better than any other teacher. Find out what it is, and use it to gain recognition for her. Have her demonstrate the talent to other teachers if it can benefit their instruction. Give her a special job or responsibility which utilizes her ability and which has status attached to it. (See "Rewarding Teachers Who Volunteer" in Chapter One for additional ways of giving teachers recognition.)

One principal solved this tale-carrying problem by having a conference with the one who carried tales and the person whom the tale involved. In the conference he asked the teacher who had spread the tale to prove the charges against the other teacher. Of course, it was an embarrassing experience because the charges could not be proved. This confrontation became known to the other teachers. It was surprising how rapidly this teacher stopped carrying tales.

Suggested Guidelines:

1. Recognize that the person who carries tales is usually seeking recognition.

2. Find ways of providing attention and status for the tale-carrier.

3. If tales are brought to you by a teacher, have a conference with the tale-carrier and the person involved. Ask the tale-carrier to prove the charges.

COMPLAINING

"One of the teachers on my staff is constantly complaining about something. If it isn't policies or procedure, it's parents or other teachers or the principal. As far as she is concerned, little is right at the school."

Complaining in a moderate degree is characteristic of human nature in general. A marked tendency to lessen the value, influence, or importance of people or things indicates a marked attitude of inferiority. By pointing out the faults of other persons the individual hopes to camouflage his own defects. Such a teacher may be seeking attention. If in the past a teacher complained and nearly every time received attention or recognition, then, for her, complaining became a pattern of behavior with strong reinforcement. To fulfill this need for attention, the teacher realizes that all she has to do is to complain. And so, she becomes a chronic complainer. But to understand her is not to excuse her, for a teacher who continually discredits or disparages the good repute and estimation of people and policies of a school is vicious. Her conduct has a deleterious effect on the other personnel and the whole school program.

Keep a record of her complaints. When you enter a complaint, record your appraisal of it—valid or invalid. Let a month go by and then call the teacher in for a conference. Say to her, "Do you know how many times you complained last month?" Present your evidence. Ask her if she is satisfied with her work. Find out the goals she has. Where is she going? Can you help her? She may accuse you of being too personal. Assure her that your interest grows out of the effect which her complaints have on the other teachers. Convince her that you are interested in having her happy in her work. Serve coffee during the conference. People are normally more relaxed and at ease over a cup of coffee. If she becomes indignant and abruptly storms out of your office, assure yourself that it was your responsibility to talk to the teacher about the problem and that as a result there will probably be a decrease in the amount of complaining by the teacher. If she remains throughout the conference, she may become vociferous. If so, listen . . . listen . . . listen . . . Above all, you do not want to argue with the teacher. When a teacher becomes angry, she may reveal some personal information about herself which will give you additional background and insights for solutions to the problem.

If you think the above action is a little too daring for you to take, assume that the teacher is striving for recognition. Provide opportunities for the teacher to gain recognition from the group. Use her assets, talents, and interests to accomplish this. In a faculty meeting, ask for her opinion on topics being discussed. Use her in special auditorium programs. She could lead the pledge of allegiance to the flag or introduce the special speaker. Sometimes seemingly insignificant things like this bring recognition to a person and adequately fulfill some urgent need. Appoint her to a committee which meets periodically to appraise and revise school-wide routines and policies. It will be unlikely that she will criticize an area in which she has borne responsibility.

Examine her complaints. Take action to remedy the valid ones. She may be more sensitive to existing problems than you are. Her complaints may help you do your job better.

Suggested Guidelines:

1. Acknowledge that moderate complaining is characteristic of human nature.

2. Recognize that excessive complaining is indicative of an attitude of inferiority, of covering up one's own defects, or of seeking attention.

3. Keep a record of the teacher's complaints and action taken.

    a. Have a conference with the teacher; present your evidence, and attempt to discover reasons for the complaining.
    b. Make a sincere effort to discover legitimate complaints if there be such.

4. Provide opportunities for the teacher to exercise leadership and provide instances in which her talents and interests will receive attention and recognition. Help the teacher to reach his goals.

5. Assign the teacher to a committee which will appraise and recommend changes in areas where his complaints are valid.

6. Take necessary action yourself to make improvements where needed.

TARDINESS

"Most of my teachers are late getting to school every morning. Some are five to ten minutes late; a few arrive just before classes begin."

This problem requires a point of view which is tempered with understanding. Teachers are professional employees and as such should enjoy the benefits of such a distinction. Like other professional people, the teacher often works many extra hours without overtime pay. If teachers were to keep an account of how much time they spend outside their normal workday preparing plans, correcting homework, serving on committees, and attending night meetings, the sum of hours would be staggering. The principal that requires strict punctuality and rigid conformity to the hours of the workday is likely to encourage teachers to take the attitude of "8:30 to 3:30 and no more."

We must remember that married women comprise a significant segment of the teaching force. Without them our teaching system would have collapsed a long time ago. These women are carrying on two full-time jobs—teacher and housewife—and it goes without saying that one of these jobs of itself carries responsibilities which are enough for any distaff member. Moreover, many of the married women are mothers. Unexpectancies occur often at rush hours, and the rush hour for a family is from the time they get up in the morning until dad kisses mom good-by, the children catch the school bus, and mom, with her books and materials tucked under one arm and the baby who is to be delivered to the baby-sitter held by the other arm, leaves home for her other job at the little red schoolhouse.

An incidental point is that principals themselves seldom set an example in getting to school on time. When principals by their actions appear to attach little importance to punctuality, the attitude becomes a contagion.

Suggested Guidelines:

1. Tardiness is no personnel problem when principals recognize that teachers put in much unpaid overtime, that teaching is a profession, and that domestic unexpectancies are often the chief cause.

2. If the principal arrived at school early enough to greet the teachers as they arrived, teachers would probably attach more importance to getting to school on time.

LEAVING SCHOOL EARLY

"My teachers are required to stay at school a half-hour after classes are officially over. Should I permit them to leave after classes are over to keep an appointment with the hairdresser or dentist, or to catch a bus or train on Friday for the beginning of a week-end, or to go to the university for a graduate course which begins at 4:00 or 4:30?"

See the first point made under the topic "Tardiness" above because it is applicable to this problem of leaving school early. We must recognize that teachers are professionals and should be treated as such; they are not employees who "punch a clock." Leaving work early and working overtime without pay have always characterized the professional. The teacher has always had claim to the latter but somehow has infrequently been granted privileges like the former.

Going to the university for an early afternoon course should always be permitted and encouraged. Almost any course will make any teacher a better one. Should a teacher who is working on a masters or a doctorate degree be permitted to leave school early for what is often described as personal gain? Of course! Do not think of the educational growth to be reaped by the person who earns an advanced degree as "personal" gain. Think of what this additional training will do for the teacher as a member of the teaching profession. If we regard teachers as professional employees, then we as principals will vouchsafe to them the benefits which professional people have always enjoyed. A strong chain consists of strong links, and the stronger the links, the stronger the chain.

Suggested Guidelines:

1. Adopt a professional attitude toward the staff. Regard teachers as members of a profession, not employees of a "sweat shop." Permit teachers to leave school early. This is one of the benefit of professionalism.

2. Encourage high scholarship which leads to excellence in teaching

LAZY TEACHER

"A few of my teachers get lazy and don't produce as much as they could Are there certain things which a principal can do to shake them out of thei lethargy?"

Nearly everybody suffers from this trait. About the middle of th school year and especially during February in temperate zones, ther is a general lassitude, a melancholy depression, and a yearning for sprin and warm breezes. A few teachers exhibit laziness at different times c the year. Some older teachers begin to slack off; other teachers ar indolent because they have no incentive to be otherwise. The principa never visits the classrooms. He show no interest in what the teacher are doing. When a teacher does something special, there is no recognitior no praise, no mention of it. "Why exert yourself?" the teachers ask Things are dull at the school. The same thing day in and day out. Neve anything different.

These conditions seem to suggest certain remedies. If the productivit of teachers is markedly lower about the middle of the school year, perhap the spring vacation, which usually coincides with Easter, should com in February. When a principal is on his toes and supervises classroom regularly and adequately, the teachers will be alert also. More *pop* visi are needed. Get into the classrooms. Let teachers know you are intereste in what is going on. Ask questions. Pay attention to specific activities c classes, special projects, new methods, and different approaches. Notice and praise; recognize and approve; admire and inspire. Often when attention is given to something commendable going on in one teacher's room, the other teachers say to themselves, "Ah, he notices. I'll have to perk up and do something!" This is one way to get a lazy teacher moving. Praise the work of other teachers. No one likes to be slighted—particularly when recognition is being handed out.

Grade level planning with the principal and with the other teachers will promote some structure, organization, and goals for instruction. Informal competition between classrooms will spark some teachers. You may have to have a conference with the teacher and determine the cause of the laziness. Here are some suggestions to get things moving in the school: invite speakers in, have intramural sports, conduct a marble tournament, prepare for a field day, conduct seminars, and discuss innovations in education, hold panel discussions on journal articles in a faculty meeting, promote action research and let teachers lead discussions on educational topics. Make your school a place where things are happening, a school that is alive, and a school where teachers are reluctant to be absent for fear of missing something.

Suggested Guidelines:

1. Consider having the spring vacation changed to February.

2. Have a conference with the teacher; talk about reasons for his laziness.

3. Supervise classrooms adequately; schedule more impromptu visits.

4. Give credit where credit is due; admire; commend; approve; praise.

5. Use grade level planning and principal-teacher planning.

6. Initiate informal competition between classrooms.

7. Make your school an exciting and stimulating place in which to

work. Provide special speakers, intramural sports, seminars symposiums, action research, pilot studies, field trips, talent shows and various clubs to establish a dynamic program.

Undependable Teacher

"There is a teacher who when given a special assignment cannot be depended on to carry it through."

School assignments for teachers often are of an amorphous nature. Some are structureless, meaningless, insignificant, and even inane. Their purposes are ambiguous and nebulous; their outcomes doubtful and uncertain. Teachers have enough to do without being burdened with unnecessary loads. A principal should never make work assignments in the school merely so he can prove or brag that things are happening in his school. The instructional function of a teacher is taxing enough; so why sap a teacher's strength with extraneous, unimportant work? And don't fool yourself—teachers know which assignments have value and which ones do not. They detest "busy work." This could be a valid reason why many assignments go unfinished.

Arrange a conference with the teacher and discuss the problem. If the teacher is unable to give causes for his behavior, or if he declines to discuss the problem with you, some general kinds of action are suggested. Supervise the progress of the special assignments. Checking once a week or every two weeks is not enough. Follow-up the assignment twice a week; find out what has been done. What are the next steps to be taken? Are the procedures clear which the teacher has to follow to complete the assignment? Does she understand the assignment? Require brief, written progress reports.

Make assignments based on a teacher's strong points and on his interests. Perhaps the teacher never receives recognition for any extra work. I have seen this happen. A teacher will spend literally hours on a special assignment and do an outstanding job—sometimes on a voluntary basis—only to have it passed over quickly by a principal at a faculty meeting, and sometimes no recognition at all is given.

Often the efforts of an undependable teacher are markedly improved when the assignment includes other teachers or a committee. Group work, like group therapy, has a salutary effect on people. They know the members of the group are counting on them. Members of the group are not only responsible to the principal but responsible to each other. If a poor job is done or if assigned responsibilities are not done, a teacher's status in the group is adversely affected. There are other individuals for whom the group offers seclusion; a few members do all the work and others do very little. Individual assignments are beneficial for these drones.

Suggested Guidelines:

1. Hold a conference with the teacher. Attempt to find out why he is undependable.

2. Be sure that special assignments for teachers are significant in nature.

3. Supervise adequately and closely the progress of the special assignment; require periodic, written progress reports.

4. Make sure the teacher understands the problem, knows the procedures which are necessary, and recognizes the significance of the outcomes.

5. Assign projects on the basis of teachers' assets and interests.

6. Give proper and sincere recognition for assignments which are successfully completed.

7. Use group work for special projects.

8. Use individual assignments for shirkers.

LATE STARTER—EARLY FINISHER

"There's a teacher on our staff who starts classroom production about a half hour after school begins and shuts down a half hour before school ends."

That's a whole hour that is being wasted! Schedule the art, music, foreign language, or physical education teacher for the first and last periods of the day for this class.

Bell signals could be used. The programmed bell could ring fifteen minutes after the school officially begins (provide 15 minutes for lunch collections and opening exercises), and five to ten minutes before school is over. Tell the teachers the reason for the bells. You may have to talk to the teacher and explain that the class is being short-changed. A review of the time allotment for the subjects may be needed.

One principal I know makes a brief visit to each teacher in the classroom shortly after opening exercises are over. He varies his visits. The teachers don't know if he'll drop in during the first five minutes, or fifteen minutes after school starts. He has never told them the reason for his visits. He only greets them with, "How are things going?" or makes a comment about something in the classroom. Occasionally, he makes the rounds of the classrooms in the late afternoon.

Suggested Guidelines:

1. Schedule special teachers for the first and last periods of the day in such a classroom.

2. Program the school bell to ring 15 minutes after school starts, and 5—10 minutes before school ends.

3. Visit teachers in their classrooms every morning. Make occasional visits to the problem teacher in the late afternoon.

4. Talk to the teacher about the problem. Review the time allotment for the various subjects.

Leaving School Premises

"One of my teachers left the school grounds during the noon hour to do some business in town. He did not have any supervisory duties at the time; his children were on the playground under the supervision of another teacher."

Occasionally a teacher will have to leave the school grounds for some reason. Because of the heavy responsibility for children, however, it is necessary that a principal know whenever a teacher temporarily leaves the premises. Sometimes a teacher will be unable to locate the principal, or the principal may be off the premises himself. A ground rule needs to be established in the handbook. One handbook I saw recently stated teachers were permitted to leave the school grounds if they did not have responsibility for children. The principal or the school secretary and the classroom teacher nearest that teacher's classroom were to be notified before leaving and upon returning.

Suggested Guideline:

1. Include a written policy in the teachers' handbook which will ensure that several people, including the principal, will be aware of a teacher's departure and return.

Unsupervised Classrooms

"A few of my teachers sometimes leave the classroom unsupervised. They usually are in the teachers' workroom running off ditto copies, in the rest room, or in the faculty room smoking a cigarette."

While the law often states unequivocally that children are to be under the supervision of a teacher at all times, there are several ways in which teachers can fulfill this responsibility. If a teacher is in the vicinity of his classroom, he can supervise it "long distance" and check on the children occasionally. In a six room school on one level the problem usually does not exist. Every area is within earshot of another area. In large schools or in schools with two floor levels the problem is real. One solution is to bring the machines or spaces which cause teachers to leave their rooms into the proximity of the classrooms. A ditto or hectograph machine placed at the end of a corridor can service the classrooms in that wing and permit "long distance" supervision. Portable machines so placed in each wing of the school will eliminate the problem altogether, as teachers can bring the machines into their classrooms. Newer school plants have included teachers' rest rooms in each wing of the building. You may be able to convert unused space into restrooms if this is your problem. Of all the reasons for leaving a classroom, going to a restroom would be strongly defensible if something of a serious nature happened while the teacher was out of the classroom. Since schools have only one faculty room, smoking can be permitted in the faculty restrooms, or in a room which is not being used by children. If a teacher has to leave the classroom and is unable to supervise it "long distance," then the teacher next door should be asked to keep an eye on the class. Teachers whose rooms are adjacent or join each other often team up and reciprocate favors with each other. The arrangement is a good one.

A principal who thinks that a teacher should never leave the classroom probably is lacking in understanding of human nature. Even teachers who are consistently good planners sometimes during the instructional day need to run off copies from a ditto master, get some materials from the storeroom, have a smoke, or just get away from the children for a few minutes.

Suggested Guidelines:

1. Permit "long distance" supervising.

2. Provide portable copying machines for the teachers in each long corridor or section of the building.

3. Designate unused rooms in each section of the building as smoking rooms.

4. Convert unused spaces to faculty restrooms.

5. Encourage teachers to assist each other in supervising children when they have to leave the room.

Telephone Calls

"My teachers abuse the rule which states that teachers are to fill out a telephone slip when personal telephone calls are made for which a toll is charged."

Suggested Guidelines:

1. Prohibit personal telephone calls on the school's telephone line.

2. Have a pay telephone booth installed.

3. Install locks on the telephones.

CARS IN PLAY AREAS

"Sometimes a teacher or a parent will drive a car into the playground area while children are playing."

Some elementary schools have become, dimensionally, so elongated and spread out that driving as close as one can to an entrance saves walking four or five hundred feet. However, the rule that no cars shall be in the playground area when school is in session is inviolable. Usually this violation occurs in the morning before school officially begins, but it can happen any time during the school day.

Usually only a temporary barricade is needed. Some schools use six or eight carpenter's "horses" to block a restricted area. Other schools use a chain combined with a lock. If "horses" are used, a sign stating the area is closed between certain times is needed; otherwise the barricade may be removed. Since teachers often bring much material to school, some of which is very heavy, the policy that they will have to arrive a few minutes early so they can unburden themselves before the barricade goes in place should be strongly established.

Suggested Guidelines:

1. Set up some kind of barricade; carpenter's horses and a chain with a lock are commonly used.

2. Put up signs stating the hours when the area is closed.

PARKING

> *"Some of my teachers park wherever they want to park. They park in front of entrances, block loading platforms, and sometimes make it impossible for school buses to make turns on the parking lot."*

There is one simple way to prevent parking problems at schools; this is giving every one a reserved space. Paint enough parking spaces for your staff and number them. At the beginning of each school year, let the teachers draw their parking space number from a hat. If the school has two parking lots, you will assign parking lots according to the location of a teacher's classroom. Include a marked area for visitors near an accessible main entrance.

Suggested Guidelines:

1. Paint and number parking spaces on the macadam. At the beginning of each school year have the teachers draw their reserved spaces, or assign spaces according to classroom location.

2. Provide a marked area near a main entrance for visitors.

TEACHER WHO SWEARS AT CHILDREN

> *"A few parents have occasionally complained about one of my teachers who now and then uses a swear word with children."*

The use of swear words is wrong; nobody can really dispute this. It is wrong for teachers to use these words in front of children or at children. It is wrong for adults to use them with adults. For some people, however, a healthy, verbal "Damn it" seems to be therapeutic. It relieves the pressure. It's a kind of safety valve.

Talk to the teacher; tell him about the complaints. Ask him to go easy, to be careful not to use swear words. But after you tell him this, you should tell him something else, because his use of swear words has perhaps told you something about him, and it is something very positive. He has become so concerned about a child or the children that his reasonable use of the language was affected. When do most reasonable people swear? Only after a bitter disappointment, when they are angry, or during frustration. The children could have caused the teacher to be disappointed, angry, or frustrated. He could care enough for the children to get upset over something they did. So tell him you understand that teaching children is a difficult task. It's frustrating, and it takes patience. Tell him you understand the problems children can be. Tell him you appreciate the interest and concern he has for the children.

Often the problems of home affect the emotional state of teachers on the job. Sometimes fatigue and lack of sleep are important contributory factors affecting emotional stability. Viewing the late show on TV can easily do it. Since teaching is so demanding, it is imperative that a teacher's body, mind, and spirit be in good condition. Everybody has a bad day now and then, though. If the teacher has a good record, I would be inclined not to do more than mention the complaint to him and ask him to be careful of his language. Other and stronger action would have to be taken if the use of improper language becomes a regular speech pattern.

Suggested Guidelines:

1. Tell the teacher about the complaints, and ask him to be careful; firmly ask him to stop the practice.

2. Sympathize with him. It takes enormous patience to teach some children.

3. Emphasize that teachers have to be in good physical and mental condition to teach children.

DRESS

"One of my teachers wore brightly colored plaid slacks to school. I knew she was having a picnic outside in the afternoon with her class, but I thought she should have worn appropriate clothing in the morning and changed into the slacks for the picnic."

A handbook for teachers is probably the most effective way of handling the "dress" problem. Not only is dress sometimes a problem with members of the teaching staff, but children also occasionally wear shorts and clamdiggers to school. Encourage teachers to help set the standards, then spell out appropriate dress in the teachers' handbook by stating what is acceptable and unacceptable dress for teachers and children. Be flexible, however; both teachers and children should be permitted to dress according to the activity in which they are participating.

If the problem persists, use an indirect approach. In the presence of the offender, compliment the specific item of dress of another staff member whom you know the offender admires. Attitudes of dress, like other attitudes, are changed by the example set by people we admire. If the indirect approach fails to bring about the desired change, then a tactful, direct approach is necessary. Do not have another teacher talk to the offender about the problem; the problem is your responsibility. When the offender is a woman and the principal is male, it is suggested that the principal discuss the problem with his wife or a close woman friend, since women know more about acceptable feminine apparel.

Suggested Guidelines:

1. The school staff, with the principal, should develop standards for dress.

2. Standards for dress should be stated in the handbook and should include specific statements about over-exposure, appropriate fit, and suitability of dress to classroom work.

3. Compliment the appropriate dress of a teacher whom the offender admires.

4. As a last resort, use a direct, tactful approach when there is a flagrant disregard of appropriate dress for the classroom.

SMOKING

"I have a couple of teachers who leave their classes to go to the faculty room for a smoke."

Although it has been over fifteen years since the writer has smoked, he can still remember the pleasures of the habit. Many employees are permitted unrestricted smoking on the job. Teachers belong to that group of workers who must alter their smoking habits to fit the job. If principals concede that smoking is pleasurable, that discomfort and tension occur when a teacher does not get a cigarette within a reasonable time when the desire arises, then by logic it can be deduced that the teaching of the teacher who smokes is affected one way or another. From my experience teachers with the greatest need usually leave their classes only once in the morning and once in the afternoon (in addition to recess times) for a smoke. For these teachers, a cigarette is a "must." If the principal has any reservations about teachers taking a quick smoke, let him, if he is an inveterate smoker, try to restrict himself to smoking before school begins, at morning recess, noon-hour, and afternoon recess. While a teacher takes a smoke, supervision can be done at "long distance" or a colleague next door can keep watch on the classroom.

It appears that some of the school policies on smoking have been in need of revision for some time. Smoking is practiced by a large majority of the people from all walks of life; yet a teacher must not permit children to see him with a cigarette in his hand although his breath and tobacco-stained fingers reveal the habit. Activities done secretly invariably call forth increased interest and curiosity. The writer questions what influence this "secret practice" by teachers is having on children and asks if teachers should not be able to smoke in front of children, just as parents, clergymen, and other respected adults do.

Suggested Guideline:

1. Permit teachers to take occasional five-minute breaks for smoking. After they have a smoke, their teaching will probably be more effective.

FACULTY ROOM

"Some of my teachers are always in the faculty room: in the morning before school officially begins, at short periods during the day, at lunch time, and after the last class ends in the afternoon."

To some teachers the faculty room is the most important room in the whole school, for it serves as a reservoir of relief from classroom routine. Teachers regard this room as the place where they can get their second wind, as a den and a hideaway, a place to let their hair down, eat a snack or smoke a cigarette, a place to let off steam about those darn kids or stretch out and nap on the couch, and most importantly, as the one room in the school building which is off limits to their darling brats.

As a principal, I would be more concerned if the staff did not use the faculty room because this could reveal teacher-teacher antipathies, personality conflicts, or lack of sincere friendliness among staff members. While children are adorable, teaching is still a difficult job, a job which has many tensions and headaches. Anybody that has a job in a room with thirty or more boys and girls, each with more energy and dynamism than the teacher, needs some respite during a day. Most faculty rooms are merely "holes in the wall." Since this is the room which benefits teachers in so many varied ways, it is imperative that the room be pleasantly decorated, furnished, and equipped. Paint the walls a soft hue and hang some attractively framed pictures, provide comfortable chairs and sofas, include hassocks and ash trays, equip it with a coffee pot and a cold drink dispensing machine, decorate it with some artificial flowers, and provide some varied current magazines. Make the faculty room a place where teachers will want to come. Do not worry if they spend some time in it. This room pays handsome dividends when the teacher returns to the classroom to teach.

Suggested Guidelines:

1. View the faculty room as a "service station" where the human dynamo gets a "tune-up."

2. Be concerned if your teachers do not use the faculty room.

3. Make the faculty room an inviting hideaway.

SICK LEAVE

"Every year some of my teachers take almost all of their sick leave. It seems they think sick leave is a fringe benefit which is to be used whether they are

sick or not. It's not fair to the teachers who never use much of their sick leave."

For every instance that a teacher uses or abuses sick leave, the educational program of that specific classroom is decelerated, notwithstanding the fine job most of the substitute teachers do. Special projects are interrupted and come to a standstill, adjustments have to be made by the children and the substitute teacher to each other, and valuable time is lost as the substitute tries to effect instruction from a few statements in the plan book. What can be done to discourage unethical use of sick leave? What can be done to reward healthy teachers who are rarely absent from school and to recognize teachers who do not abuse sick leave benefits?

Initiate a compensatory program for unused annual sick leave. For instance, if ten days per school year are allowed for sick leave, and Teacher A uses only one of those days, the remaining nine days would be reimbursable to Teacher A. However, reimbursement has to be set at a dollar figure which induces teachers not to take sick leave if they are marginally sick or if they want to abuse the benefit, but yet discourages actually sick teachers from coming to work in order to get the unused sick leave bonus at the end of the school year. Perhaps five dollars per day for unused sick leave would accomplish these objectives. Such a bonus program would promote continuity of the educational program, decrease significantly the expenditures required for substitute teachers, increase morale of the teaching staff by the receipt of the bonus, and effect a more equitable arrangement of sick leave benefits.

Unused sick leave, although paid for by the annual bonus, could still be accumulated according to the maximum number of days set by the school board. Subsequently, if a teacher required more sick leave than the annual sick leave maximum, he could draw on his accumulated sick leave; however, the five dollars which had been paid to him for unused sick leave in prior years would be deducted for each day used over the annual maximum sick leave. For example, if annual sick leave is ten days, and in the School Year 1963–64 Teacher A used one day of sick leave and at the end of the School Year was paid $5 per day for unused days, or $(9 \times \$5)$ $45, nine days would be accumulated by the teacher for possible use in future years. The next School Year, 1964–65, Teacher A was beset with sickness and took 17 days of sick leave. The first ten days would be charged to annual sick leave for which the teacher would receive full pay according to his salary. The next seven days for which

Teacher A was paid $5 per day at the end of the School Year 1963–64 could be used as sick leave, but $5 per day, or $35, would be deducted from his pay.

Suggested Guidelines:

1. Establish a compensatory program for unused sick leave. The amount paid for unused sick leave should only be about five dollars per day, so that teachers will be discouraged from abusing sick leave and sick teachers will be encouraged to stay home.

2. Have a dynamic school program where things are always happening, a school where teachers think they will miss out on something if they take a day off.

"I suspect that some of my teachers use sick leave for personal business."

Leave for personal business is a necessity in the modern age in which we live. When personal leave does not exist, prevarication and deception are encouraged.

Suggested Guideline:

1. Encourage the school board to adopt a policy of 1 or 2 days leave per school year for personal business.

Moonlighting

"One of my teachers works at a service station seven hours every night. A teacher from another elementary school works the 4–12 shift at the tire company."

There are usually two reasons for "second jobs:" One reason is that people need extra money to meet ordinary living expenses. The other is that people in a materialistic society continually buy more products and services than their income allows, no matter how high their salary is.

The first problem can be solved; the second is insolvable. The status of the teaching profession has been steadily rising. However, when starting salaries of firemen and policemen are compared with those of teachers, the status of the profession is more clear. What can be done about moonlighting? Should heads of households who are teaching get more money than married women or single teachers? That would be unfair, for each teacher is doing the same work—teaching children. Usually this "money squeeze" affects young men in education. Elementary education is in great need of men who are adept at teaching children. Boys in the intermediate grades urgently need to identify themselves with the masculine image. Each elementary school should have at least one man on the teaching staff. If elementary schools want men teachers, they have to offer more than what is often termed "a woman's salary." Since low teaching salaries encourage moonlighting, what can be done? There are many jobs in a school which can carry extra pay: director of audio-visuals, teacher for shut-ins, census taker, distributor of supplies, director of intramural sports, school librarian and clerk assisting with purchase orders, regular reports, and inventories. To a beginning teacher, five hundred or a thousand dollars above the starting salary usually is all it takes to give him a significant salary assistance to discourage moonlighting.

Suggested Guidelines:

1. Discourage moonlighting by providing extra duties with extra pay.

2. Continue to fight for professional salaries for all teachers.

SUMMER WORK

"The school board usually hires six to eight male teachers to paint and repair school buildings in the summer; it seems like a waste of money when you see how little some of these teachers do."

The hiring of teachers for summer work has often been advantageous to the individual and to the school board. It has also been disadvantageous to both. Often teachers have been hired for a pittance, when if they had

had time to look around for another job they could have more than doubled their pay. Sometimes the $1.25—$1.50 an hour has not paid off for the school board either, for that hourly wage has hardly provided much incentive for outstanding work.

There are other considerations for an effective summer work program. With teaching itself being so mentally enervating and fatiguing, the summer work program should not be started until a week after school officially closes (after the last day of teaching), so that all summer workers will have a chance to relax from the tensions built up while teaching. The summer work should be scheduled in writing so that when the worker completes one job he will know what the next job is. Also, two or three men should work in a group, if possible. Each member of a small group seems to motivate the other members. Often the work of two men working together is more than twice that of one man working alone. Groups of more than three workers often develop drones. Each group should have a working leader who receives extra supervisory pay. Otherwise, a problem can stalemate a group until the big boss comes around. Essential is a good hourly rate for all men; the importance of a job is often psychologically measured by the amount of money being paid.

There is much professional work which can be done in summer. Schools often fail to employ teachers in this area. But school board members whose visions are sharper and whose minds are wiser know there are functions which busy teachers can not do in a school year. Each summer selected teachers are employed to develop and revise curriculum guides, field trip handbooks, orientation brochures for kindergarten and first grade, and teacher recruitment materials.

Suggested Guidelines:

1. Begin summer work programs no sooner than one week after school is officially over; this will give workers a chance to relax from teaching tensions.

2. Pay summer workers a good hourly rate; it will influence the caliber of work the men do.

3. Use two to three workers in a group; have a leader for each group.

4. Schedule work in writing so workers know what comes next.

5. Include professional work in your summer work program.

UNETHICAL TEACHERS

"The most blatant form of unethical behavior in our school is that the teachers talk about one another, particularly in the teachers' lounge."

This behavior is common to many schools. It happens in the best of schools. It appears that some people would rather discuss a person's negative qualities than his positive characteristics. This is the nature of some humans. Professional people should have high principles and should display superior behavior patterns, if only as a result of their extended education. Such unethical behavior is not in keeping with what is expected of a professional person. The professional man remembers to "Do more building up than tearing down." He knows that if "I can't say something good, I'll say nothing at all."

What is needed is a close review of the code of ethics for teachers. Many teachers, experienced and inexperienced, are not aware that such a code exists. A close study of the code may be the first step to bury Miss Idle Gossip. Write to the state or national teachers' organization and obtain the code, and request a copy for each teacher. It will provide a firm basis for getting started on the problem. Reserve one faculty meeting for a discussion of the code.

Appoint a committee composed of a cross-section of the grade levels to appraise the ethical behavior of the teaching staff according to the code. Stress that improvement can come only when the appraisal has been honest. The committee should make specific recommendations for improving conduct. Suggest to the teachers that individual and collective responsibility are needed. *They must police it themselves.* Group pressure is always more effective than the pressure of one person. Posters and placards illustrating specific ethical and unethical behavior can be placed in strategic locations where most of the gossip and backbiting occur. You will start seeing some immediate changes. Teachers will begin to be careful of what they say and how they act, and perhaps you yourself will be a little more careful.

Suggested Guidelines:

1. Obtain the code of ethics from your state or write for the national code from National Education Association, 1201 Sixteenth St., N.W., Washington 36, D.C.

2. Discuss each part of the code in a faculty meeting.

3. Appoint a committee to appraise the ethical behavior of the staff and to make specific recommendations for improvement.

4. Emphasize that each teacher has a responsibility to adhere to high standards.

5. Stress the strength and influence of the group on deviates.

6. Ask the art teacher to paint a few posters on ethics which will be displayed at frequented locations.

7. Set the pace yourself.

TEACHER SALES TO PARENTS

"Several parents have made complaints about a teacher who solicits ency-clopedia sales from the parents of children whom she teachers."

This is unquestionably an unethical practice. Some state laws prohibit such solications by teachers in the county in which they teach. If your state does not outlaw this practice, suggest to the superintendent that the school board enact a policy.

Suggested Guidelines:

1. Suggest to your superior that a policy be established which prohibits teachers from soliciting sales in the community in which they teach.

ALCOHOLISM

"I have an alcoholic on my staff. Several times I have seen him taking a nip from a bottle."

The first question a principal should ask himself is "Is the teacher a satisfactory teacher when he is sober?" If he is, he should be given the same consideration as other ailing employees. Next, a principal can have a conference with the teacher. In the conference state that you know about his drinking and that unless it stops it will be necessary to cancel his teaching contract. A firm attitude at this point has helped many alcoholics. Do not lecture, moralize or condemn the teacher, and do not express hard feeling toward him. Ask him if he *wants* to stop drinking. If he cannot stop or does not want to stop, the teacher should be discharged. If you feel he is sincere in wanting to stop, you may suggest a definite plan of action.

Suggested Guidelines:

1. The first step is to suggest that the teacher see a doctor for physical treatment. The object is to thoroughly clean the mind and body of the effects of alcohol. You could require that the teacher present evidence that he is being treated, such as a doctor's note. In severe cases a leave of absence may be necessary.

2. Give the teacher the name, address, and phone number of an official of the nearest chapter of Alcoholics Anonymous. The teacher must undergo a change of attitude. Counselors who have had considerable experience dealing with the problem of alcoholism agree that AA is the *best* therapy existing today for the alcoholic.

3. Conduct follow-up conferences with the teacher. This will tell him you are interested in his progress and will encourage him to stay "on the wagon."

IMMORAL TEACHERS

"It is strongly rumored that there is a teacher on my staff who is morally loose and leads a wild social life."

Nearly all teaching contracts make it possible to dismiss a teacher on the grounds of immorality. One or more conditions have to be met before action is taken. When a principal adheres closely to these conditions, he protects himself from grave charges of slander or libel. The conditions are: the principal observes an immoral act by the teacher; the principal has an unimpeachable witness to an immoral act by a teacher; a parent brings a charge of immorality on behalf of a child; or a charge of immorality is written in the newspaper. There can be, of course, slightly different variations. When any one of these conditions obtains, there is only one step to take. The teacher must be suspended immediately. If the charge is proved valid, the teacher must be dismissed. To permit a teacher of proven disrepute in this area to continue in the employ is to flagrantly misuse the delegated power which the members of the community give to its electees on the school board. Regardless of the specific immoral act, which can include exhibitionism, prostitution, sex orgies, adultery, fornication and sodomy, the crux of the question is: How much confidence can parents have in an immoral teacher who instructs their children? What is the moral influence of such a teacher on the children? Would you want your child to be taught by an immoral teacher? The answers are obvious.

Suggested Guidelines:

1. Before action is taken, the principal must either observe the immoral act, have an unimpeachable witness to the immoral act, weigh the evidence which a parent presents on behalf of a child, or read the account of the immoral charge in the newspapers. The principal consults his superiors immediately for approval and direction in taking suspension action.

2. If the charge of immorality is a valid one, there is no alternative but to dismiss the teacher.

3. If the charge can not be substantiated and the source of the original information was a person, you should inform him of the results of your investigation.

CHRONIC DEBT

"A young teacher on the staff must be heavily in debt. Her creditors call the school often. How can I help her?"

It is not unusual for firms that extend credit to call the borrower's place of employment in the hope that the employer will bring additional pressure on the borrower to put his financial business in order. Young teachers like young graduates in other field often display inexperience in sound financial management and get in debt over their heads. Young teachers, especially those away from their families, need understanding and are usually willing to accept guidance from the principal. Pressure on a teacher, financial or otherwise, can affect her morale and consequently her effectiveness as a teacher.

The first step for the principal is to tell the teacher that he is aware that creditors are calling the teacher at the school. This will take the pressure off. Tell her that you understand the financial problems of beginning teachers, that you experienced financial pressures yourself when you first got out of college. Inform her about the techniques of unscrupulous money lenders. Tell her how they operate. Tell her they cannot bring charges against her if she regularly pays any amount off the balance. Offer your help and advice. She will probably take it because such a person is usually in need of some advice.

Here is an account of how one principal helped a beginning teacher with this problem. A plan for paying off the debts was developed by the principal and the teacher. The principal called each creditor and told him that he, the principal, and the teacher had a plan which would ensure that the balance would be paid off in regular installments. The principal and the teacher together planned a budget for the teacher. They told each creditor what monthly payment would be paid on the balance due. The creditors were not to call the teacher at school, and thus the threat of notifying the supervisor about the teacher's delinquency was eliminated. All correspondence between the creditors and the teacher was to be made to the principal. Each month the teacher drafted the necessary checks and turned them over to the principal with the prepared envelope. After making a record of each payment, the principal mailed the checks. This procedure continued until all the debts were paid. The principal then gave the teacher all the correspondence between the loan companies and himself.

Usually older teachers do not have serious financial problems. If one does, the initial step a principal can take is to tell the teacher that he will notify the loan companies not to call the teacher at the school. This will eliminate the threat of the debt affecting her job security. Since older teachers are reluctant to discuss their financial problems with anyone, give her assurance that her personal debt is her personal business. Do not offer any advice—just let it go at that. She is probably embarrassed over the whole matter, thinking that after all these years she has not learned to manage her own financial affairs. When you take the above action, however, you give her confidence and trust in you. Later, she may come to you with the problem and ask for help.

Suggested Guidelines:

1. Recognize that nearly every one has financial problems of one kind or another. Young teachers away from home are vulnerable to advertising and can easily overextend themselves.

2. Steps in helping the young teacher:
    a. Tell the teacher you are aware that creditors are calling her at the school.
    b. Assure her you will notify the creditors not to call her at the school.
    c. Inform her about the techniques of loan sharks and other creditors.
    d. Offer her assistance with the problem.
    e. Develop a plan and budget for paying off the debts. Supervise the regular monthly payments. Notify the creditors that the teacher is not to be called at the school. Give her understanding and sympathy.

3. Steps in helping the older teacher:
    a. Tell the teacher you are aware of the problem and that her personal debt is her personal business.
    b. Notify the creditors not to call her at the school.

7

Non-Professional

Personnel Problems

Hire wreckless bus drivers, employ filthy cooks, entrust the pressure of boilers to sleeping custodians, combine this with a sensuous secretary and you will be lucky if within a month you are not filling out employment applications. Any one of these conditions by itself can cause you serious trouble. The lives of the children are more dependent on these non-professionals than they are on the teachers—a fatal bus accident, food poisoning, or a boiler explosion just as examples. Yet the author acknowledges that the principal can have many pleasant associations with these people. One of the finest compliments I ever received was from a custodian who told me when I was leaving the school how much he appreciated the talks we had in his office.

When the photographer comes to your school to take pictures, have the nonprofessional staff photographed, individually and as a group. The photographs are usually free and the staff will appreciate your thoughtfulness. Display these portraits with complimentary captions in the display case at the entrance to the school.

If problems arise in the bailiwick of the non-professional staff, be sure the worker's opinions are given proper consideration and weight, for it is they, the workers, who know more about the aspects of their job than anyone else, and they have to live with these decisions. Decisions in conflict with their suggestions should be discussed with them; the rationale for the decision should be given.

CONFLICT BETWEEN TEACHER AND NON-PROFESSIONAL

"Some of my teachers take the liberty to ask or tell the custodian to do certain custodial jobs in the classroom. The custodian has told me he resents having so many bosses, and besides he doesn't have time to do some of the things teachers ask."

The relationship of the professional staff to the non-professional staff has to be firmly established. Both staffs come under the direct supervision of the principal. Neither staff is subordinate to the other. The non-professional has authority over his assigned duties and the equipment in his care. The professional staff has direct responsibility for the children. If children are misbehaving, the teacher has the authority to discipline and manage them. This authority and the management of children is never shared with the custodian, the secretary, or the cafeteria workers. The bus driver has a few prerogatives in dealing with children. The custodian does not order, suggest, or tell children or teachers to do certain things. If he has complaints about children or teachers, he makes his report to his superior, the principal.

The non-professional has direct responsibility for the area of his work. If the children have occasion to be within these confines, the professional staff will abide by the policies and procedures which have been set by the non-professional, and the teachers will directly supervise the boys and girls. The authority and management of the non-professional's area of work are never shared with a teacher. The teacher does not order, suggest, or tell the non-professional to do certain things. If a teacher has complaints about the way non-professionals do their work, he takes them to his superior, the principal.

All work orders for teachers come from the principal. All work orders for the non-professional staff likewise come from the principal. Develop a custodial request form which teachers can use and turn in to the office. These requests are entered in a log-book, and the request form is initialed (approved) by the principal and given to the custodian. The request form is checked, dated, and signed for by the custodian when the job is completed, and it is turned back to the office where the log-book entry is similarly checked as completed. The request form is then filed. If this procedure is followed and the afore-mentioned principles of authority are honored there will be little friction between the teachers and the non-teachers in the building.

Suggested Guidelines:

1. The immediate superior of both the professional and non-professional is the principal.

2. Neither teachers nor non-professionals share their duties or responsibilities with each other.
   a. The teachers have direct supervision of children.
   b. The non-professional has direct supervision over the obligations of his areas of work.

3. All complaints by either teachers or non-professionals are made to the principal.

4. Rules of thumb:
   a. General school policies and procedures are honored by non-professionals.
   b. Teachers honor the prerogatives of non-professionals in their bailiwick.

5. *All* teacher requests for custodial service are submitted in writing, entered in a log-book, approved by the principal, assigned to the custodian, completed, signed for, and returned to the office by the custodian, checked-off in the log-book, and filed.

BUS DRIVERS

"The problem I have with bus drivers is dealing with their complaints that the children make too much noise on the bus and that some children seriously misbehave."

Someone has said that the bus drivers have the most difficult and the most unrewarding job connected with the education of children. After six hours of confinement, some intermediate children, particularly, break loose, bent on doing all those things which they could not do while they were in school: yell, eat, grab, slap, punch, push, pull, swear, change seats, stand up, talk back to safeties, ridicule the driver, use obscene gestures, and many other accompanying offenses.

Bus safety is imperative. It is about time principals stopped coddling misbehaving children on the school bus. The lives of all the other children, the bus driver, passengers and drivers of other vehicles, and pedestrians are jeopardized by the fourth, fifth, and sixth grade boys on some public school busses. Left unchecked, these offenders set the example which will be repeated by first, second, and third grade boys in just a few years.

The minor offenses can be taken care of by the teachers assigned to the busses, but dealing with children who repeatedly misbehave on the bus is the principal's obligation. The first action is preventive. Ann Hoppock of the New Jersey State Department of Education has prepared a monograph* on this topic in which she makes these suggestions: if possible, teachers should travel to and from home on the school bus and teach children to be courteous and self-controlled; children in any grade can dramatize bus-safety practices such as walking to the bus stop, standing in line, waiting to cross the road until the bus and the traffic have stopped, and riding on the bus; murals can be painted which show different situations calling for safe bus behavior. She states that a good relationship between the children and the bus drivers can be developed early in the school year. The children and teachers can invite the bus drivers to come to the school and discuss bus safety. Each group of children can meet with their own bus driver. The children can develop the rules for riding busses. The children learn to respect the drivers. The drivers think a little differently about the children who want to help them with their job. After three months, another meeting could be planned for evaluating the bus safety program.

If a few children repeatedly and seriously misbehave, the principal should take appropriate remedial action. Notify the parents and discuss solutions with them. Also, let them know that if Johnny continues to

*Anne Hoppock, "If Your Children Travel By Bus," *School Health Education*, 22: No. 2, pp. 6–7, Newark, N.J.: New Jersey Tuberculosis League, Inc., November–December, 1948.

misbehave, then for the safety of the children riding the bus, of other people in cars, and of pedestrians, they will have to provide private transportation for Johnny to and from school. This declaration is usually sufficient for most parents to help you correct the child. One effective solution for you is to have Johnny report to you each morning after he gets off the bus. Give him an index card with dates to report to you. He reports to you personally to discuss his bus behavior. Have him report each day of the first week, every second day the second week, every third day during the third week, and gradually taper off his brief conferences with you, if his behavior improves. Tell the boy you are periodically checking his behavior with the bus driver, which you will do.

When I was a teacher there were five or six boys whose bus misbehavior was seriously recurrent. Finally, in desperation I sat down and thought long and hard; proper arrangements were made and one day, after school, the boys and I visited the state police barracks, the city hospital, and a mortuary. This experience helped the boys to understand the gravity of the problem. An improvement in their behavior occurred over-night.

If the child still misbehaves after initially contacting the parents, you will have to tell the parents that the boy cannot ride the bus for one week, after which he will be given one more chance. If he continues to misbehave after being deprived of bus transportation, you have no alternative but to bar him from riding the bus.

Suggested Guidelines:

1. Lend firm support to the bus drivers in their attempts to promote safety on the busses.

2. Promote proper bus behavior for the children in your school by obtaining films on bus safety, inviting policemen to discuss bus safety, and encouraging teachers to ride the busses.

3. Suggest that teachers use dramatizations, mural paintings, and discussions to teach safety.

4. In the early part of the year invite bus drivers to meet and discuss bus safety with the children who ride their busses; the

children can formulate safety rules. Conduct an evaluative meeting with the drivers and children early in the school year.

5. Notify the parents of serious offenders, and develop with them the action which the two of you as partners will take to solve the problem.

6. Follow-up children who misbehave by having them report regularly to you.

7. Bar children from riding the school bus if remedial action does not bring improvement in their behavior.

Cooks

"What can be some of the problems of cafeteria workers?"

I have had few actual problems with these workers. Occasionally they have complained that teachers do not adequately supervise their children in the lunch line and cafeteria hall or that the lunch count was late. But in the main the relative freedom which they have in their area has been supported by responsible efforts. If visitors eat in the cafeteria, always introduce them to the cafeteria workers on the serving line. This is just good etiquette. These people are part of the team, too.

You will want to insist on high standards of cleanliness in terms of physical plant and equipment, in the preparation of food stuffs, and in the grooming of workers. Require that finger and hand cuts be bandaged and that the worker change bandages frequently when working around food. Because of an unclean bandage which absorbed the poison from a cut on a cafeteria worker's finger, many children at one school were made ill. Require annual physical examinations for cafeteria workers. Chest x-rays should also be annually taken.

Suggested Guidelines:

1. Introduce visitors to the cooks and cafeteria workers.

2. Insist on high standards of cleanliness: floor, equipment, preparation of food stuffs, and grooming of workers.

3. Require that first-aid bandages for cuts be changed frequently.

4. Require the use of hair nets for women workers.

5. Require annual physical examinations and chest x-rays for all workers.

CUSTODIANS

"What are some guidelines for avoiding problems with the custodial force?"

First, each custodian should be given a job description sheet on which are listed the duties performed daily, weekly, monthly, semi-annually, and annually. This makes his job easier. He only has to check the list to see what has to be done. Any special jobs, like arranging rooms for night meetings, should always be in writing; this helps him to remember. Provide a small bulletin board in the custodian's office onto which notices can be tacked.

No matter how competent your custodians are, conduct *weekly* inspection tours of the grounds and plant with them. Even good workers tend to slacken off when their boss fails to supervise them adequately. Carry a clip board and list things which need attention. Date the inspection and have the custodian sign both copies. Give him one copy which he will return to the office when all items have been completed. File the other copy, and take it with you for follow-up on the next week's inspection.

There is always work to be done around the school. Be sure your custodians keep busy. Give them a 15 minute rest period in the morning and afternoon and assign them a space for an office. Clarify their position in the school: that they have no authority over children or teachers, and that teachers have no authority over them; that any work orders will come to them approved by you; that any complaints about children or teachers are to be brought to the principal. Also emphasize that they are to be appropriately groomed each day. When you take visitors on a tour of the school, be sure you introduce the custodians to them—introduce them as **Mr.** John Doe—and at the same time add a compliment about the contribution the custodian makes to the cleanliness of the school. To be introduced to visitors gives the custodian a sense of importance, and the compliment will make him glad that you recognize his efforts.

Some custodians are proficient in sports. If you ever play sports outside with the youngsters—and occasionally you should—invite him to play on one side and you play on the other. This small consideration of his ability in sports will increase the respect he has for you. It will foster mutual admiration and respect between the children and custodian. The children will be interested in helping the custodian to do his job at the school.

Occasionally invite the custodian to your office for a cup of coffee or a coke and a chat. Stop by his headquarters sometimes—don't give him the impression that you are arrogantly superior. Talk his language— sports, weather, his interests. The custodian is an important person; he talks to many people in the community, and some listen to his opinions. Therefore it is wise to develop a good work relationship with him for the benefit of the school.

Suggested Guidelines:

1. Schedule the custodian's work and give him a copy; give him notices of special jobs in writing.

2. Conduct weekly inspection tours, no matter how competent he is. Give him a written copy of the items which need attention; this he will return to the office when completed.

3. Discuss the concept of his having no authority over children or teachers, and of no teachers having authority over him; all work orders come to him from you; complaints about children and teachers come to you from him.

4. Introduce visitors to the custodian; praise him in front of them for jobs well done.

5. Include him in some outside games with you and the children.

NURSES

"How can I keep the nurse busy? Is it proper to assign the nurse jobs which don't directly concern her training?"

A large elementary school requires a full-time nurse. It is not the personnel problems of the nurse—which are rare—that are important. Rather, the problems of significance are related to the work-load of nurses. It is my opinion that nurses are being used in less productive ways than their training permits. There are nurses that spend nearly all of their time in the health room, often doing nothing more than receiving patients, weighing and measuring children, administering audiometer examinations, and completing health records. A nurse's job is more than this. We can determine a nurse's function by agreeing that school health consists of areas of prevention, remedy, and instruction. The nurse can contribute to each of these areas. She can procure and distribute pamphlets and flyers on common diseases. She can arrange individual and group meetings for parents of children from deprived and poverty-stricken areas. She can promote the allotment of funds from the P.T.A., other local organizations, or the school board for dental, orthidontal, and medical work for indigent children. The classroom teacher can often use the nurse to clarify and extend the instruction in health education. If we make a judgment that a nurse is needed full-time in the school, as with any other employee, we, as the supervisors, have the responsibility to develop a job description which will justify the taxpayer's expenditure. It is neither proper nor professional to delegate clerical jobs to the nurse when there are innumerable untapped areas of school health needs to which the nurse by her training and experience can contribute.

Suggested Guidelines:

1. Appraise the work-load of the school nurse; develop a job description which includes using her training and experience for prevention, remedy, and health instruction. Some suggestions are:

   a. Procuring and distributing flyers on disease and illness.

   b. Investigating home conditions which need attention; providing individual and group counseling for parents on problems of diet, cleanliness, clothing, and sanitation.

   c. Reporting to the proper health authorities conditions in the school community which she is unable to correct or do anything about.

   d. Chairing a committee which seeks out families in need of clothing and food stuffs; making collections for the indigent.

   e. Establishing detection programs for classroom teachers which identify children who need dental or medical treatment.

   f. Promoting the allotment of funds from organizations for dental programs and for special problems requiring audio, ocular, medical or dental treatment.

   g. Supplementing, clarifying, and extending the classroom health education program by discussing pertinent topics with classes.

   h. Providing assistance to the principal for ascertaining areas of the school building where health conditions should be improved.

   i. Sponsoring the safety patrol and overseeing its activities.

SECRETARIES

"What are some of the problems which principals have with secretaries?"

The problems which a principal has with the secretary are in three categories: her work-load; her relationships with children, staff, and the public; and the secretary-principal relationship. One of the easiest ways to have the services of a secretary curtailed is to have her sit in the office with nothing to do. It is the obligation of the principal to assign work to her. Many of the routine reports of the principal can be prepared by the secretary, thus freeing him for classroom visitations. Inventories, correspondence, filing, typing letters and purchase orders, and mimeographing are a few of the jobs that are plentiful around the school. If the secretary has some extra time, she can relieve the teachers of some of their clerical functions. The secretaries of some schools do all of the work connected with attendance registers. The teachers only send to the office each morning the names of the absent children. Other secretaries type and mimeograph materials for the use of the teachers in their instruction. Give her a job description in which her duties are listed. When you leave the school for a convention or summer vacation, be sure you leave a list of things—more than she can get done—so she will be busy during your absence.

The second area of possible trouble is the secretary's relationship to children, staff, and the public. This area covers her ability to do her job well while getting along with people. Although she must demonstrate a liking for children, she must exercise no control or authority over them. It is important that she relate satisfactorily with the staff, but she cannot entertain the slightest notion that she is second in command. She must get along with people exceptionally well. She must possess poise and be a good listener, because her shoulder will be used by many teachers to cry on. Parents, teachers, and the non-professional staff, especially when the principal is not available, will share their complaints, insults, accusations, allegations, and anger with her. In the course of her work she will become familiar with confidential information about the staff. The secret information she possesses—whether positive or negative—must not affect the way she interacts with these people. She must be diplomatic with teachers who try to entice her to reveal secrets. She must be an able person, well groomed at all times, pleasant in appearance and voice, alert, and adept at handling people and machines. Above all, she must be a responsible person who is not discouraged by her lack of authority.

The last area of concern is the secretary-principal relationship. Take especial care here, particularly if you are married. You and she may never have had an affair in your lives and may never entertain the idea of having one, but sometimes mere proximity has a subtle effect on two people. So exercise propriety and discretion in all your relationships with her. Your job and future are too important to be cast to the winds because of careless indiscretion. Don't give people any reason to instigate rumors. Treat the secretary professionally. If your office door is not plate glass, keep it open when you dictate to the secretary in your office. If you are easily tempted, employ a middle-aged woman as your secretary.

Suggested Guidelines:

1. Keep the secretary busy. Give her a job description sheet. Relieve the teachers of some clerical work by assigning it to the secretary. Give her sufficient work to do when you are away from the building.

2. Point up to your secretary the importance of certain aspects of her job: confidentiality; relationships with children, teachers,

non-professional staff, and parents; voice and grooming; no authority over children, teachers, or non-professional staff; a good listener.

3. Exercise caution in your relationship with the secretary; seldom shut your office door when she is in your office; seek an experienced middle-aged secretary if you are tempted by slim ankles.

Index

Index

179